Fruits of the Soul 2

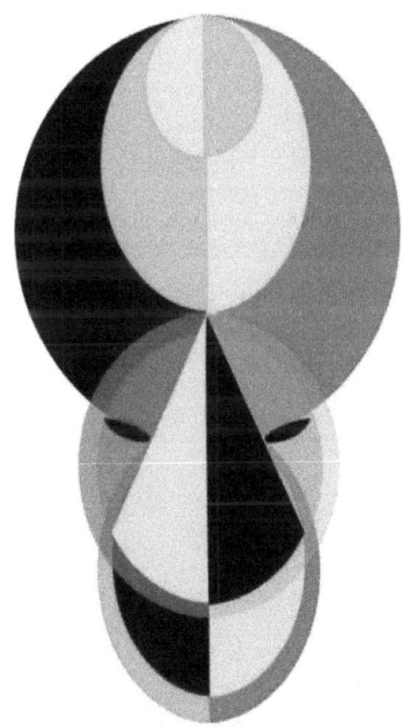

A THINK DOCTOR PUBLICATION
www.thinkdoctorpublications.com

COPYRIGHT NOTICE

If copyright material has been inadvertently used without permission, acknowledgement or credit, the editors and publisher will be more than happy to make the necessary arrangements for such concerns to be addressed at the first possible opportunity.

ISBN: 9781943274512

"MAUDIE"

&

"RASHADA"

"THE SIMMS, SMITH AND DIXON FAMILY

ABOUT THE EDITOR

D. Constantine-Simms is an Occupational Psychologist and Counselling Psychologist and a qualified Therapeutic Career Coach, and regularly contributes to:

http://thinkdoctorcareercoaching.blogspot.co.uk

PAPERBACK BOOKS AUTHOR

Constantine-Simms has previously edited the following books:

- Fruit of the Soul 1 (2015)
- Rice & Peas For The Soul 4 (2015)
- Rice & Peas For The Soul 3 (2015)
- Rice & Peas For The Soul 2 (2015)
- Rice & Peas For The Soul 1 (2014)
- The Greatest Taboo: Homosexuality in Black Communities (2001)

- Hip Hop Had a Dream: Vol. 1 The Artful Movement (2008)
- 12 Years A Slave
- Behind The Scenes
- Thirty Years A Slave,...
- Incidents in the Life of a Slave...
- Fifty Years In Chains
- From Bondage To Freedom
- Hearts and Minds (Vol. 1)
- Hearts and Minds (Vol. 2)

E-BOOKS BY AUTHOR

- How to Get Motivated
- How to Plan For A New Career
- How to Develop Unstoppable Confidence
- Successful Interviews: Making The Most Of The Interview

- The Interview Guide: A Job Interview Is No Different Than Finding The Right Partner
- The Structure and Application of Cognitive Behavioural Therapy
- How to Think Critically
- Mentoring As A Workforce Development Strategy
- The Counselling Process In Six Stages: A Basic Guide For Psychologists Counsellors and Psychotherapists
- Linking Emotional Intelligence To Effective Leadership
- Stress Management
- A Critique Of Executive Coaching Through The Psychodynamic Window
- Otto Kernberg's Theory of Personality: Pathological Narcissism and Borderline Personality Disorders

- Personality Development and Confidence Building
- The Psychology of the Courtroom
- How To Improve Your Communication Skills
- How Employment Assessment Centres Work
- Effective Presentations Skills
- Linking Emotional Intelligence To Effective Leadership
- Stress Management Leading Career Development and Employability
- The History of Psychological Testing
- How To Have A Bad Interview
- Have You Ever Thought of Becoming A Life Coach
- Successful Interviews
- The 360 Degree Feedback System Tool By Far.

TABLE OF CONTENTS

INTRODUCTION

The Fruit of the Soul 2 is a collection of more than 50 inspirational stories based on the biblical term "Fruit of the Spirit" which sums up the nine visible attributes of a true Christian life, which are love, joy, peace, patience, gentleness, goodness, faith, meekness and temperance. ***Fruit of the Soul 2,*** will show that when any who speaks of the work of the "Holy Spirit", they are speaking about the operations of the Spirit of God in the material world we live in, and within us. The heart wrenching stories in this book also highlight the fact that God the Holy Spirit isn't here just to hang out, or to do a miracle for sport, or bliss someone out for an hour or so. The Spirit is there to cause things to happen in peoples' lives that bring them more in tune with God's purposes on earth (and beyond). When the Spirit starts changing someone, it shows as a growth in character, a change in their way of life that is good for the people they live among. They start actually being the person of love God calls us to be. This change in character and way of life breeds 'fruit of the Spirit', like the fruit grown by a tree can feed people and wildlife. From ancient times to today, abundant fruit from an orchard is seen as cause for hope and celebration. Abundant spiritual fruit of the soul also breeds hope and is well worth celebrating as the stories in this book suggest.

Have a great read and God Bless

IT'S HOW YOU SEE IT

A blind boy sat on the steps of a building with a hat by his feet. He had a sign which read: "I am blind. Please Help." There were only a few coins in the hat. When a man came walking by, he took a few coins from his pocket and dropped them into the hat. Then he took the sign, turned it around, and wrote some words on the back. He put the sign where it was, so that everyone who walked by would see the new words. Soon the hat began to fill up. A lot more people were giving money to the blind boy. That afternoon the man who had changed the sign came to see how things were going. The boy recognized his footsteps and asked, "Were you the one who changed my sign this morning? What did you write?" The man said, "I only wrote the truth. I said what you said but in a different way. I wrote:

'Today is a beautiful day, but I cannot see it.'"

Both signs told people the same thing... that the boy was blind. But the first sign simply said the boy was blind. The second sign told people they were extremely fortunate that they were not blind. Should we be surprised that the second sign was more effective?

Moral of the Story:

Be thankful for what you have. Be creative.
Be innovative. Think differently and positively.
When life gives you a reason to cry, show life that you have 100 reasons to smile. Face your past without regret. Handle your present with confidence. Prepare for the future without fear .Keep the faith and drop the fear... just remember God is Near!

FRESH FISH

A fisherman set up a stall to sell fresh fish to tourists visiting a fishing harbour. In front of his new stall, he placed a large board displaying the words, 'FRESH FISH SOLD HERE' to attract prospective buyers. Several customers came to buy fish from his stall. One of his customers made a suggestion, "The board is large and readable. But it is too long.

The word 'HERE' is unnecessary as the board is quite close to the stall. It may be deleted to make the board short and sweet." The seller found that the suggestion was logical. So he erased the last word. Now the board read, 'FRESH FISH SOLD'.

Later another customer gave a novel suggestion: "The word, 'SOLD' is not needed on the board as fishes are displayed here for sale and not for exhibition." The seller agreed and deleted the word, 'sold.' Now the board read 'FRESH FISH.'

Sometime later, a new customer examined the board and gave his opinion, "The word 'FRESH' need not be displayed publicly as you sell only fresh fish and not rotten fish. It is an insult to other sellers in this area." The seller readily agreed and modified the board. It now had only one word, 'FISH.'

Another person visited the stall after sunset. He said, "The smell of your fish can be felt all around this stall. I had no difficulty to locate it though your board was not clearly visible in the dim light. It is not essential to place the board, 'FISH' here." The seller accepted the suggestion and removed the last letter from the board. The next day, his business was dull. New customers could not identify the stall easily as the board was blank. They went to other stalls in the area.

The fisherman's fate was the result of responding to every suggestion from others. People are lavish in showering advices and critical comments. We must apply our wisdom to identify the relevant, reasonable and acceptable advices.

The Holy Bible is the Word of God. We can learn it by prayerful reading and by regular and systematic study. Authoritative books and qualified persons may be consulted to clear our doubts and gain more insight. False interpreters of the Bible are very common. They may visit us and misdirect our faith by misinterpreting the Word of God. They act as the messengers of Satan. We must have correct concepts and convictions about our Faith.

Then nobody can mislead us. St. Paul cautions us against false prophets who misinterpret the Holy Scriptures and try to misdirect the faithful believers, "I say this because there are some people who are upsetting you and trying to change the Gospel of Christ. But even if we or an angel from heaven should preach to you a gospel that is different from the one we preached to you, may he be condemned to hell!

We have said it before, and now I say it again: if anyone preaches to you a gospel that is different from the one you accepted, may he be condemned to hell!" {Galatians 1: 7-9}.

THE SNEEZE

They walked in tandem, each of the ninety-two students filing into the already crowded auditorium. With their rich maroon gowns flowing ... and the traditional caps, they looked almost as grown up as they felt. Dads swallowed hard behind broad smiles, and Moms freely brushed away tears.

This class would NOT pray during the commencements - not by choice, but because of a recent court ruling prohibiting it.

The principal and several students were careful to stay within the guidelines allowed by the ruling. They gave inspirational and challenging speeches, but no one mentioned divine guidance and no one asked for blessings on the graduates or their families. The speeches were nice, but they were routine ... until the final speech received a standing ovation. A solitary student walked proudly to the microphone. He stood still and silent for just a moment, and then, it happened.

All 92 students, every single one of them, suddenly SNEEZED!!!!

The student on stage simply looked at the audience and said, "GOD BLESS YOU, each and every one of you!" And he walked off stage ...

The audience exploded into applause. This graduating class had found a unique way to invoke God's blessing on their future with or without the Court's approval. This is a true story; it happened at the University of Maryland.

THE STORM

After a few of the usual Sunday evening hymns, the church's Pastor slowly stood up, walked over to the pulpit and, before he gave his sermon for the evening, briefly introduced a guest Minister who was in the service that evening.

In the introduction, the Pastor told the congregation that the guest Minister was one of his dearest childhood friends and that he wanted him to have a few moments to greet the church and share whatever he felt would be appropriate for the service.

With that, the elderly gentleman stepped up to the pulpit and began to speak.

"A father, and his son, and a friend of his son were sailing off the Pacific coast," he began... "When a fast storm blocked any attempt to get back to the shore. The waves were so high, even though the

Father was an experienced sailor, he could not keep the boat upright and the three were swept into the ocean as the boat capsized." The old man hesitated for a moment, making eye contact with two teenagers who were, for the first time since the service began, looking somewhat interested in his story. The aged minister continued with his story...

"Grabbing a rescue line, the father had to make the most excruciating decision of his life: to which boy would he throw the end of the life line?

He had only seconds to make the decision.

The father knew that his son was a Christian and he also knew that his son's friend was not. The agony of his decision could not be matched by the torrent of waves. As the father yelled out 'I Love You, Son!' he threw out the life line to his son's friend. By the time the father had pulled the friend back to the capsized boat his son had disappeared beneath the raging swells into the black night. His body was never recovered," the old man said sadly. By this time, the two teenagers were sitting up straight in the pew, anxiously waiting for the next words to come out of the old Minister's mouth. "The father," he continued, "knew his son would step into eternity with Jesus and he could not bear the thought of his son's friend stepping into an eternity without Jesus. Therefore, he sacrificed his son to save the son's friend. How great is the love of God that he should do the same for us? Our Heavenly Father sacrificed His only begotten Son so that we could be saved. I urge you to accept His offer to rescue you and take hold of the life line He is throwing out to you in this service." With that, the old man turned and sat back down in his chair as silence filled the room. The Pastor again walked slowly to the pulpit and delivered a brief sermon with an invitation at the end. However, no one responded to the appeal. But, within moments after the service ended, the two boys were at the old man's side. "That was a nice story," politely stated

one of the boys, "but I don't think it was very realistic for a father to give up his only son's life in hopes that the other would become a Christian."
"Well, you've got a point there," the old man replied, glancing down at his worn Bible. As a big smile broadened his narrow face, he looked up again at the boys and said, "It sure isn't very realistic, is it? But I'm here today to tell you this story gives me a glimpse of what it must have been like for God to give up His only Son for me. You see...I was that father, and your Pastor is my son's friend."

EMAIL FROM HEAVEN

One day, God was looking down at Earth and saw all of the rascally behavior that was going on. He decided to send an angel down to Earth to check it out. So, he called one of His angels and sent the angel to Earth for a time.
When he returned, he told God, "Yes, it is bad on

Earth; 95% are misbehaving and 5% are not."

God thought for a moment and said, "Maybe I had better send down a second angel to get another opinion." So God called another angel and sent him to Earth for a time too.

When the angel returned he went to God and said, "Yes, it's true. The Earth is in decline; 95% are misbehaving and 5% are being good."

God was not pleased. So, He decided to e mail thc % that were good, because He wanted to encourage them; give them a little something to help them keep going.

Do you know what that e-mail said?

No?

Oh, so you didn't get one either?

Your own special place, And have my family around ME. To be taken seriously when I talk. I want to be the centre of attention and be heard without interruptions or questions.

I want to receive the same special care that the TV receives even when it is not working. Have the company of my dad when he arrives home from work, even when he is tired. And I want my mom to want me when she is sad and upset, instead of ignoring me. And I want my brothers to fight to be with me. I want to feel that family just leaves everything aside, every now and then, just to spend some time with me.

And last but not least, ensure that I can make them all happy and entertain them. Lord I don't ask you for much. I just want to live like a TV.'

At that moment the husband said 'My God, poor kid. What horrible parents!' The wife looked up at him and said 'That essay is our son's !!!'

LOVE AND MADNESS

A long time ago, before the world was created and humans set foot on it for the first time, and vices floated around and were bored, not knowing what to do. One day, all the vices and virtues were gathered together and were more bored than ever. Suddenly, Ingenious came up with an idea: "Let's play hide and seek!" All of them liked the idea and immediately. Madness shouted: "I want to count, I want to count!" And since nobody was crazy enough to want to seek Madness, all the others agreed. Madness leaned against a tree and started to count: "One, two, three..." As Madness counted, the vices and virtues went hiding. Tenderness hung itself on the horn of the moon...

Treason hid in a pile of garbage...

Fondness curled up between the clouds...and

Passion went to the centre of the earth....

Lie said that it would hide under a stone, but hid at the bottom of the lake... whilst

Avarice entered a sack that he ended up breaking.

And Madness continued to count: .... "Seventy nine, eighty, eighty one..."

By this time, all the vices and virtues were already hidden - except Love. For undecided as Love is, he could not decide where to hide. And this should not surprise us, because we all know how difficult it is to hide Love. Madness: "...ninety five, ninety six, ninety seven..."Just when Madness got to one hundred.........Love jumped into a rose bush where he hid. And Madness turned around and shouted: "I'm coming, I'm coming!"

As Madness turned around, Laziness was the first to be found, because Laziness had no energy to hide. Then he spotted Tenderness in the horn of the moon, Lie at the bottom of the lake and Passion at the centre of the earth. One by one, Madness found them all - except Love.

Madness was getting desperate, unable to find Love. Envious of Love, Envy whispered to Madness: "You only need to find Love and Love is hiding in the rose bush."

Madness grabbed a wooden pitch fork and stabbed wildly at the rosebush. Madness stabbed and stabbed until a heartbreaking cry made him stop.

Love appeared from the rose bush, covering his face with his hands. Between his fingers ran two trickles of blood from his eyes. Madness, so anxious to find Love, had stabbed out Love's eyes with a pitch fork.

"What have I done? What have I done?" Madness shouted. "I have left you blind! How can I repair it?"

And Love answered: "You cannot repair my eyes. But if you want to do something for me, you can be my guide." And so it came about that from that day on, Love is blind and is always accompanied by Madness.

Keep smiling,

ZEN OF LIFE

Avoid negative sources, people, places and habits.

Believe in yourself.

Consider things from every angle.

Don't give up and don't give in.

Everything you're looking for lies behind the mask you wear.

Family and friends are hidden treasures, seek them and enjoy their riches.

Give more than you planned to.

Hang onto your dreams.

If opportunity doesn't knock, build a door.

Judge your success by what you had to give up in order to get it.

Keep trying no matter how hard it seems.

Love yourself.

Make it happen.

Never lie, steal or cheat.

Open your arms to change, but don't let go of your values.

Practice makes perfect.

Quality not quantity in anything you do.

Remember that silence is sometimes the best answer.

Stop procrastinating.

Take control of your own destiny.

Understand yourself in order to better understand others.

Visualize it.

When you lose, don't lose the lesson.

Excellence in all your efforts.

You are unique, nothing can replace you.

Zero in on your target, and go for it.

Love, Light, Blessings

GOD'S MESSAGE TO WOMEN

When I created the heavens and the earth, I spoke them into being. When I created man, I formed him and breathed life into his nostrils. But you, woman, I fashioned after I breathed the breath of life into man because your nostrils are too delicate. I allowed a deep sleep to come over him so I could patiently and perfectly fashion you.

Man was put to sleep so that he could not interfere with the creativity. From one bone I fashioned you. I chose the bone that protects man's life.

I chose the rib, which protects his heart and lungs and supports him, as you are meant to do. Around this one bone I shaped you. I modeled you. I created you perfectly and beautifully. Your characteristics are as the rib, strong yet delicate and fragile. You provide protection for the most delicate organ in man, his heart. His heart is the center of his being; his lungs hold the breath of life. The rib cage will allow itself to be broken before it will allow damage to the heart. Support man as the rib cage supports the body.

You were not taken from his feet, to be under him, nor were you taken from his head, to be above him. You were taken from his side, to stand beside him and be held close to his side. You are my perfect angel. You are my beautiful little girl. You have grown to be a splendid woman of excellence, and my eyes fill when I see the virtues in your heart. Your eyes – don't change them. Your lips how lovely when they part in prayer. Your nose, so perfect in form, your hands so gentle to touch. I've caressed your face in your deepest sleep; I've held your heart close to mine. Of all that lives and breathes, you are the most like me.

Adam walked with me in the cool of the day and yet he was lonely. He could not see me or touch me. He could only feel me. So everything I wanted Adam to share and experience with me, I fashioned in you: my holiness, my strength, my purity, my love, my protection and support.

You are special because you are the extension of me. Man represents my image – woman, my emotions. Together, you represent the totality of God. So man – treat woman well. Love her; respect her, for she is fragile. In hurting her, you hurt me.

What you do to her, you do to me. In crushing her, you only damage your own heart, the heart of your Father, and the heart of her Father.

Woman, support men. In humility, show him the power of emotion I have given you. In gentle quietness show your strength.

In love, show him that you are the rib that protects his inner self. Did you not know that WOMAN was so special in God's eyes? Now we really know! Hallelujah!!

I SAW HIM IN CHURCH

I saw him in the church building for the first time on Wednesday. He was in his mid-70's, with thinning silver hair and a neat brown suit.

Many times in the past I had invited him to come to church. Several other Christian friends had talked to him about the Lord and had tried to share the good news with him.

He was a well-respected, honest man with so many characteristics a Christian should have, but he had never accepted Christ, nor entered the doors of the Church. "Have you ever been to a church service in your life?" I had asked him a few years ago. We had just finished a pleasant day of visiting and talking.

He hesitated. Then with a bitter smile he told me of his childhood experience some fifty years ago.

He was one of many children in a large

impoverished family. His parents had struggled to provide food, with little left for housing and clothing.

When he was about ten, some neighbors invited him to worship with them. The Sunday school class had been very exciting! He had never heard such songs and stories before!

He had never heard anyone read from the Bible! After class was over, the teacher took him aside and said, "Son, please don't come again dressed as you are now. We want to look our best when we come into God's house." He stood in his ragged, unpatched overalls.

Then looking at his dirty bare feet, he answered softly, "No, ma'am, I won't-ever."

"And I never did," he said, abruptly ending our conversation. There must have been other factors to have hardened him so, but this experience formed a significant part of the bitterness in his heart. I 'm sure that Sunday School teacher meant well. But did she really understand the love of Christ? Had she studied and accepted the teachings found in the second chapter of James?

What if she had put her arms around the dirty, ragged little boy and said, "Son, I am so glad you are here, and I hope you will come back every chance you get to hear more about Jesus."

I reflected on the awesome responsibility a teacher or pastor or a parent has to welcome little ones in His name. How far-reaching her influence was!

I prayed that I might be ever open to the tenderness of a child's heart, and that I might never fail to see beyond the appearance and behavior of a child to the eternal possibilities within.

Yes, I saw him in the church house for the first time on Wednesday. As I looked at that immaculately dressed old gentleman lying in his casket, I thought of the little boy of long ago. I could almost hear him say, "No, ma'am, I won't-ever."

And I wept.

THE TALKING TWINS

A popular story, originally composed by Útmutató a Léleknek in Hungarian, depicts the fictitious conversation between two twins in their mother's womb. One is an atheist (named A) and his brother is a believer (named B). The believer told his atheist brother that he felt that there is an end to their life in the womb and after the present period in the womb, they will be born into a different environment, where they can enjoy a more joyful and meaningful life. His atheist brother rejected the idea and argued that their stay in the wonderful world of the womb would continue forever and provide them with infinite and endless pleasure.

He held in his hands the umbilical cord and said that it would supply them food for ever.

He denied the possibility of a birth and a life after birth. He refused to accept the existence of a mother whom he has not seen in person with his own eyes. But the believer argued that the cord belongs to a loving mother who provides them with all their needs and that he was longing to see his mother in person after his birth.

He told that they could hear the sweet voice of their mother and feel her tender love if they remain quiet and silent for some time.

He explained that they live within her and owe their existence to her love and mercy. He was sure that his most merciful mother would look after their needs even after birth and continue to love them beyond measure. Days passed and one day they were born. They opened their eyes to witness a new, bright, brilliant, beautiful, and wonderful world.

They saw and felt their mother and her tender loving care. She held them close to her heart and fed them. They knew that they were safe in her affectionate arms. Life after death is a reality. In the heaven of happiness reserved for the righteous, we will meet our loving Lord who created us to be with Him forever. St. Paul teaches about life after death, "I consider that what we suffer at this present time cannot be compared at all with the glory that is going to be revealed to us" {Romans 8: 18}.

"What can be seen lasts only for a time, but what cannot be seen lasts forever" {2 Corinthians 4: 18}.

"What no one ever saw or heard, what no one ever thought could happen, is the very thing God prepared for those who love Him" {1 Corinthians 2: 9; Isaiah 64: 4}.

THE PLIGHT OF A KITE

A boy was flying a colorful kite in an open space on a windy day. By careful and skillful manipulation of the string attached to the kite, he could raise it from the ground. Strong winds raised the kite to greater heights. The boy was glad to see his kite soar up into the sky. His friends watched his work with wonder. A small bird was attracted by the kite's swift movements. The bird challenged the kite for a race to reach still greater heights. The kite silently followed the bird but became almost stationary at a stable height. The bird flew back to investigate the cause of the kite's unexpected halt. The bird was surprised to see that the kite was being pulled by a boy towards him using the string fastened to the kite. As the bird was not aware of the kite's mechanism of ascent and stability, he assumed that it was caught in a trap and that the boy was trying to capture it. The silly bird decided to rescue the kite from its plight and snapped the string by a sharp bite with his sleek beak and set it fully free. But the kite lost its balance, control and stability. Descending haphazardly following the wind and gravity, it landed on a tall tree.

The bird was surprised to see the kite entangled in the branches of the tree and cried aloud, inviting it to resume the race. Seeing no response, the bird left the scene, wondering about the fate of the kite.

The pull on the string is the driving force behind the kite's ascent and stability. But to an ignorant person, the string may appear to hamper the progress of the kite. Adverse conditions in life have a similar role in shaping our personality and destiny. It is said that adversity is the best university for our education and training. Our life is stabilized by the pull of several strings. The teachings of our religion and Holy Scriptures, the whisper of our conscience to follow the righteous path, the instructions of our parents, the state and society are the strings holding us in a stable state physically, mentally, emotionally and spiritually. Let us learn that these are not bonds restricting our freedom or hindrances to our progress. They are essential for our smooth and sustained progress to perfection and sanctity. Freedom is not the right to do as we please, but the liberty to do what we ought to do. Rules are framed to make our freedom full and fair. Voluntary sacrifice of personal rights is the basis of peaceful social life. There is no liberty without limitations; no freedom without responsibility. Commandments of God and the laws of our Nation do not curtail our freedom; they make our liberty a reality. Cicero said, "We are in bondage to the law in order that we may be free." St. Peter advises, "Live as free people; do not, however, use your freedom to cover up any evil, but live as God's slaves" {1 Peter 2: 16}. St. Paul warns us, "Be careful, however, not to let your freedom of action make those who are weak in the faith fall into sin" {1 Corinthians 8: 9}. "As for you, my brothers, you were called to be free.

But do not let this freedom become an excuse for letting your physical desires control you. Instead, let love make you serve one another" {Galatians 5: 13].

THE BLIND BEGGARS

The Gospels narrate the miraculous curing of a blind beggar by Jesus at Jericho {Mark 10: 46-52; Luke 18: 35-43}. St. Mark identifies him as Bartimaeus, the son of Timaeus. He was sitting by the side of the road when he heard that Jesus was passing by the road. He cried out in excitement, "Jesus! Son of David, take pity on me!"

The people scolded him and asked him to be quiet. But he shouted more loudly. Jesus stopped and called him. Bartimaeus threw off his cloak, jumped up and came to Jesus. Jesus asked him, "What do you want me to do for you?" He replied, "Teacher, I want to see again." Jesus consoled him, "Then see! Your faith has made you well." He was cured of his blindness instantly. Then he followed Jesus, giving thanks to God. There is an interesting legend about Bartimaeus, which has been depicted in plays and a film. When Jesus summoned him, in the excitement, he had left his cloak, walking stick and the beggar's bowl full of coins, by the roadside.

Jumping with joy after the miraculous recovery, he distributed the coins in the bowl among the beggars and went to meet his nearest friend, another blind beggar who was still begging by the side of the busy road. Bartimaeus was eager to have his friend restore his sight like him. He narrated how Jesus cured him mercifully and asked his friend to approach Jesus who was still at Jericho and receive the gift of sight from Him. Quite unexpectedly, his friend refused the proposal.

He thought about his early years and replied firmly, "I do not wish to see this thankless world again!"

Then he narrated his bitter experiences following the loss of his vision. He loved his family dearly and had made great sacrifices for his wife and children. But they rejected him as a useless burden when he became blind. They sent him away from his home and he had to become a beggar to earn his livelihood. He was in agony when he remembered those painful moments in his life.

Finding that his mission had failed, Bartimaeus sadly bid farewell to his blind friend and returned to Jesus to be His faithful follower forever.

A meaningful presentation in the 'Shalom Television' depicted a principled priest who accepted the invitation of a wealthy man to bless his home. Reaching the house, the priest put on his holy vestment and started the formal prayer. Suddenly he noted that the old father of the person was not to be seen anywhere. The priest enquired.

The person replied reluctantly that he had shifted his ailing father to an asylum for the aged, as the old man was a burden to his busy life. The priest stopped the ceremony, closed the prayer book and removed the vestment. He declared firmly that he would continue the blessing only after the head of the family was brought back to the house. He counselled the members of the family.

His wise words convinced them that their action was cruel and wrong.

They hurried to the old age home, met the old father, begged his pardon and respectfully escorted him back to their home. They informed the priest who readily returned to complete the blessing.

He reminded them that God has designed the family in the likeness of Heaven. He quoted the words of Jesus delivered after the transformation of Zacchaeus, "Salvation has come to this house today" {Luke 19: 9}.

The Bible teaches, …"Respect your father and mother, so that you may live a long time in the land that I am giving you" {Exodus 20: 12}.

"God's curse on anyone who dishonours his father or mother" {Deuteronomy 27:16}. "If you curse your parents, your life will end like a lamp that goes out in the dark" {Proverbs 20: 20}."Honour your father with all your heart, and never forget how your mother suffered when you were born.

Remember that you owe your life to them. How can you ever repay them for all they have done for you?" {Sirach 7: 27, 28}.

PEARL FROM PAIN

The 'pearl oyster' is a marine bivalve mollusc of the family 'Pteriidae'. It has a natural procedure to protect itself from foreign substances. Occasionally, by an accident, a foreign particle such as a grain of sand or a parasite may gain entry into the inner body of the oyster between the mantle and the shell causing great discomfort, irritation and possibly, pain to the oyster. 'Nacre' is the mineral substance secreted by the mantle of the oyster to fashion the shell. As the oyster is unable to expel the intruding foreign body, it initiates a natural defensive reaction. The mantle secretes 'nacre', the smooth, hard, crystalline mineral, layer upon layer around the irritant intruder to coat it and cover it completely.

In course of time, the covered irritant becomes a beautiful, silky, lovely and lustrous gem called a pearl. It has a shimmering iridescence and a special inner glow not found in other types of gems. The coating of nacre consists of microscopic crystals of calcium carbonate, aligned perfectly with one another so that light transmitted along the axis of one crystal is reflected and refracted by another to display a spectacular spectrum of light and colour.

A similar situation may arise in our life frequently. Our mind may be hurt and wounded by adverse conditions and the unkind behaviour and harsh words of others. When we are ignored, rejected, misunderstood or ill-treated by prejudice or hatred, our mind gets wounded. By trusting in the infinite love of God, we can let Him cover our wounds and sorrows by several layers of his healing love.

Like the pearl made in the oyster from the healing wound, we too can develop precious pearls of peace, strength and sanctity in our mind and soul by the soothing and sanctifying grace of God.

It is said that adversity is the best university to perfect our personality. We must accept the sufferings and pain of life with the spirit of sacrifice. In life, troubles, suffering and failures may fall on us. Let us not worry about them or feel helpless or hopeless. We should not let the troubles defeat us or bury us. Let us use every failure as a stepping-stone and not as a stumbling-block. Our life is like a boat, sailing through the sea of the world. We may be threatened by the tempests of troubles, tribulations and temptations. But we can sail safely if our faith is strong. God has control over the forces of nature. He may give us tests and trials so that we may grow further and stronger, but he never abandons us during hard times. God is with us in our joys and tears throughout our life. "The Lord says…I alone know the plans I have for you, plans to bring you prosperity and not disaster, plans to bring about the future you hope for" {Jeremiah 29: 11}.

SELECTION OF STUDENTS

Socrates (469-399 BC) was a great philosopher and teacher of ancient Greece. Several young men approached him with the request that they may be accepted as the students of Socrates. The great teacher performed a simple test to select the suitable students. He asked the aspirants to look into a pond and report to him what each of them had seen in the pond. Most of them said that they had seen their own image in the still water. Socrates sent them away as unqualified to be his students.

A few of them reported that they had seen fishes swimming around in the still water. Socrates gladly admitted them to his school. When asked about this test by his senior disciples, he said that those who saw their own image in the water were in love with their own ego and so were useless as students.

An egoist or egocentric person is preoccupied with

and considers only his own interests, welfare, pleasure, advantage and advancement.

He acts with only himself and his own interests in mind. He puts his own interests and needs first in every action without any concern for others.

He is self-centered and selfish and thinks too much about oneself and too little about others.

Egotists are boastful and think and talk too often or too much about oneself. They have a very high sense of self-importance. "The Lord hates everyone who is arrogant; He will never let them escape punishment" {Proverbs 16: 5}. "Pride leads to destruction, and arrogance to downfall" {Proverbs 16: 18}. "No one is respected unless he is humble; arrogant people are on the way to ruin" {Proverbs 18: 12}. "Happy are those who are humble; they will receive what God has promised" {Matthew 5: 5}.

"For everyone who makes himself great will be humbled, and everyone who humbles himself will be made great" {Luke14: 11}. St. Paul advised, "No one should be looking to his own interests, but to the interests of others" {1 Corinthians 10: 24}.

He advised the Philippians, "Don't do anything from selfish ambition or from a cheap desire to boast, but be humble towards one another, always considering others better than yourselves. And look out for one another's interests, not just for your own" {Philippians 2: 3,4}. In his farewell speech to the elders of Ephesus, St. Paul said, "I have shown you in all things that by working hard in this way, we must help the weak, remembering the words that the Lord Jesus himself said, 'There is more happiness in giving than in receiving" {Acts 20: 35}.

BITTER HALF

Socrates, the great Greek philosopher, had a nagging and quarrelsome wife, Xanthippe. One day she shouted furiously at Socrates and his friends. Finding no reaction, she got into a violent temper.

She picked up a bucket full of washing water and poured it on the head of Socrates. He remarked with a smile, to his friends, "We know that a thunder will be followed by a rain!" Later, he advised a young man, "By all means, marry. If you get a good wife, you will become happy. If you get a bad one, you will become a philosopher." A recent cartoon depicted the most effective seat belt for a husband driving with his wife in the other seat in the front.

It effectively covers the wife's mouth while supporting him. Its advantage is that it lets him drive without her interference! The teacher of biology in a school distributed plantlets to all the students with instructions to plant them near their home, look after the growing plants regularly and observe their condition every day. All the students except one reported that the plants were growing steadily. One student complained that his plantlets refused to grow. The teacher questioned him and discovered the reason. The boy was in the habit of examining the roots of the plants every day after pulling them out of the soil in order to assess the growth of the plants. Obviously, his idiotic over-enthusiasm had deprived the plant of an essential condition for steady growth - lack of disturbance! An over-enthusiastic and highly religious lady was worried that her husband was a heavy drinker. She used to torment him by her constant complaints and unnecessary advises. With much effort, she managed to bring him to a Charismatic convention. After informing the organizers, she occupied a seat close to her husband's seat and was continuously disturbing him, expressing irritation whenever he showed any sign of sleep or restlessness.

She frequently complained to the priest that her husband was not attentive. The priest finally told her sternly, "Please occupy a seat in a different place and leave him alone. Tell more about him to God and less about God to him. It is God's grace and not your presence that will transform him. "Let us add to every prayer the words taught by Jesus in the 'Lord's prayer'. He taught His disciples, "May your will be done on earth as it is in heaven" {Matthew 6: 10}. Several families maintain peace by surrendering to the dominance of the stronger partner. Real happiness results only when there is close co-operation and mutual respect between partners. Otherwise the better half becomes the bitter half. In several oriental Christian churches, during the sacrament of matrimony, the priest adorns both the husband and the wife with the matrimonial ring. It symbolizes that the spouse is received from God. Matrimony is thus a union of three - the husband, wife and God. Marriages are conceived in heaven and celebrated on earth. The ideal family is an image of heaven.

PESTERING PARTNERS

A sick man was brought to a hospital by his pestering wife. She was very dominating and talkative. The doctor examined the patient in detail. But the wife was a constant disturbance, annoying him by her persistent pestering. Finally the doctor told the man, "You badly need some rest. I shall prescribe a sedative drug (sleeping pill). Give it to your wife." God created man in His image. Then he instituted the family in the image of heaven, hoping that it would be a heaven of happiness. But pestering partners often make it a hell of horror. Referring to women who harass their husbands with petty annoyances and repeated demands, an exist said humorously, "God created Adam first. Then He slept, pleased with His creation. Then He created Eve. From that day both God and Adam lost their sleep!" God formed Eve from a rib of Adam. It is said that God did not choose a bone from the head or foot of Adam to make Eve, with a very good intention. If she was made from a bone from his head, she would claim superiority and try to be his boss.

If she was made from a bone from his foot, he would have tried to be her boss, suppress her and treat her as his slave.

Creating a partner from a rib which is close to the heart implies that the partners are equal before God and have equal rights and responsibilities to make their family a heaven of happiness. They should render hearty support to each other even
during disappointment, disability, discomfort, distress, disease or disaster. Matrimony is a sacred sacrament, a source of divine grace. Marital partners participate in God's act of creation. Their attitudes and actions should be complementary and not contradictory.

There is a legend about the return of the Holy Family after the exile in Egypt. They reached a junction and could not locate the correct route to Nazareth. They sought the guidance of a youthful young man, but he got angry, cursed them and walked away without providing any help.

Then they approached another young man who gladly guided them and even accompanied them to make sure that they reached Nazareth safely.

St. Mary asked child Jesus about the best reward for the two young men. Jesus said, the first person who was bad-mannered should receive a saintly and good-natured wife who would correct him and transform him.

The kind, compassionate and considerate man should get a bad-mannered wife so that he can transform her by his sanctity. Dave Meurer said, "A great marriage is not when the 'perfect couple' comes together. It is when an imperfect couple learns to enjoy their differences."

Euripides (484 BC - 406 BC) said, "Man's best possession is a sympathetic wife." St. Paul teaches,

"Every husband must love his wife as himself, and every wife must respect her husband" {Ephesians 5: 33}.

FOOLISH FRIENDS

A rabbit and two ducks were intimate friends. They used to meet on the bank of a river and have detailed discussions. One day the ducks told the rabbit that they had found a carrot farm on the other bank of the river. The rabbit was excited and sought the help of his friends to cross the river, reach the farm and relish the carrots. The ducks agreed to carry him across the river.

They devised an ingenious plan to cross the river. The two ducks entered the river and stayed close to each other. The rabbit carefully mounted on their back and stayed still, placing his forelimbs on one duck and his hind limbs on the other duck. Then the ducks slowly swam across the river, staying close to each other. The rabbit cautiously balanced his body on top of the moving birds.

As they reached the centre of the river, the ducks saw a large number of fishes swimming together.

In the excitement of finding a delicious meal in the shoal, the ducks quickly swam to either side to catch the prey. They forgot about the poor rabbit who fell down into the deep river as the ducks moved away. The ducks remembered their mission only after they finished their feast. But, by that time the rabbit had drowned.

The foolish ducks were sorry to miss their dearest friend. They cursed their crazy craving for food. The Book of Proverbs in the Holy Bible advises, "Keep company with the wise and you will become wise.

If you make friends with stupid people, you will be ruined" {Proverbs 13: 20}.St. John advises, "My children, our love should not be just words and talk; it must be true love, which shows itself in action" {1 John 3:18}. Jesus taught us, "My commandment is this: love one another, just as I love you. The greatest love that a person can have for his friends is to give his life for them" {John 15: 12, 13}.

CROSSING THE CHASM USING A CROSS

A man had to endure a lot of trials, troubles and tribulations in his life. In a moment of deep depression he asked God why he was constantly being exposed to suffering and pain. God answered his question in a dream. He saw a large crowd of people moving forward towards heaven along with him. Each person was carrying a wooden cross. Later he examined his cross and found that it was longer than the crosses carried by many of his fellow travellers. He wanted to lessen his burden. He saw a saw on the way. Happily he cut away a large portion of the main leg of the cross using the saw. He marched forward faster with a lighter load in a better mood. The heaven of happiness was seen at a distance. He moved fast to reach his destination at the earliest. Suddenly he saw a chasm, a deep crack or opening in the ground before him.

His colleagues were seen to place their crosses across the cleft like a bridge and easily walk along the cross to cross the chasm. Their crosses were of the correct length to cross the fissure. But his shortened cross was too short to help him.

He stood alone, helpless and hopeless, while all others easily crossed the chasm using their own crosses and rushed to reach the Promised Land.

He lamented that he had blocked his path to glory by foolishly shortening his cross.

Life is not a bed of roses but a path of thorns.

God gives us burdens; and He also gives us shoulders! We are like tea bags. Our strength is revealed only when we get into hot water! Stumbling blocks and stepping-stones differ only in the way we use them.

ADVERSITY IS THE BEST UNIVERSITY.

William Arthur Ward opined, "Adversity causes some to break; others to break records." He said, "Great men rise above adversity and attain new heights of achievement by turning tribulations into triumphs, failures into fortunes, setbacks into successes, obstacles into opportunities, and burdens into blessings. They refuse to be hampered by handicaps, dismayed by discouragements, overcome by opponents, defeated by disappointments, or destroyed by disasters." Jesus said, "Whoever does not take up his cross and follow in my steps is not fit to be my disciple" {Matthew 10: 38, Luke 14: 27}."If anyone wants to come with me, he must forget self, carry his cross, and follow me" {Matthew 16: 24, Mark 8: 34, Luke 9: 23}. St. Paul says, "I consider that what we suffer at this present time cannot be compared at all with the glory that is going to be revealed to us" {Romans 8: 18}.

A LOVING LION

The legend of Androcles and the lion has undergone several modifications through ages. It was adopted by Aesop in his famous fable where Androcles is portrayed as a fugitive slave who ran away from his cruel master and befriended a wounded lion which later refused to harm him. In his famous play, 'Androcles and the Lion' (1912), George Bernard Shaw (1856-1950) presents Androcles as a compassionate Christian tailor who was saved in the Roman amphitheatre by the lion he once nursed. The following is a variant version of the old legend. A king was influenced by the priests of pagan gods. They considered the Christians as their enemies because the Christians refused to worship idols and preached against idolatry. The pagan priests conspired against the Christians and inspired the king to issue an order that everyone must worship the idol of the king in public and offer incense and sacrifices as acts of adoration to the king. Anyone who refused to adore the king's idol publicly was to be thrown into an arena before a hungry lion.

The king's army was ordered to arrest anyone who refused to adore the king and bring the culprit before the king for trial and judgment. Hundreds of Christian martyrs were killed by the king's lions and thousands of people used to gather around the arena to enjoy the public massacre.Fierce lions were captured from the forest by the hunters appointed by the king and kept in strong cages in the palace. They were starved before being let loose in the fenced arena into which the helpless Christians were thrown down mercilessly amidst the applause of thousands in the gallery around the arena. Androcles was identified as a practising Christian and was chased by the king's armed guards. He escaped into a dense forest and sought refuge in a cave. A wild lion with a large thorn stuck in its right paw entered the cave, limping on three legs and crying in great pain. He raised the swollen paw and showed it to Androcles who examined it with great care and compassion. He carefully removed the thorn and applied the fresh juice of medicinal herbs to alleviate the pain and cure the wound. The lion felt relieved and licked the hands of Androcles as a mark of gratitude and love. He wagged his tail like a tame dog and left the cave thankfully. A few days later, the king's men traced Androcles and captured him. He was produced before the king. As Androcles refused to renounce his Christian faith, the king ordered that he shall be thrown to be eaten by a wild lion in the arena the next day. Thousands arrived to witness the cruel murder. The king and the queen were seated in a special box. Androcles was brought to the arena. He knelt down and prayed to God fervently. A hungry lion was brought in a cage in a carriage. Its heavy grating was opened and the lion was let free to attack the helpless Androcles. The hungry lion jumped from the cage into the arena, roaring fiercely; ready to pounce upon his prey. But, quite unexpectedly the lion became tame as he approached Androcles. He wagged his tail and licked Androcles with great affection. The lion recognized Androcles as the person who removed the thorn from his painful paw and affectionately nursed him before the lion was caught from the forest and was taken into the custody of the king's troops. Everyone was struck with wonder. The king learned from Androcles the story of his encounter with the lion and praised his kindness. The king was deeply impressed by the religion of Androcles which enabled him to show mercy and love even to animals. The king stopped the persecution of Christians and allowed Christians to practise their religion with full freedom. Androcles was appointed as an important officer in the king's palace but he thankfully declined the offer and devoted his life to care for the poor, the sick and the illiterate people of his country. Jesus said, "And now I give you a new commandment: love one another. As I have loved you, so you must love one another. If you have love for one another, then everyone will know that you are my disciples" {John 13: 34, 35}. "Happy are those who are merciful to others; God will be merciful to them! Happy are the pure in heart; they will see God!" {Matthew 5: 7, 8}.

JESUS AND JUDAS

A story is told about a famous painter who went in search of suitable models with the traits of the characters in the Lord's Last Supper to paint his masterpiece. He identified an innocent-looking young member of the cathedral choir as model to represent the features of kindness, compassion, goodness, innocence and tenderness of Lord Jesus. He sat as model while the painter painted the figure of Jesus. Later he completed the figures of the eleven apostles except Judas Iscariot. Years went by but he was still in search of a model for Judas Iscariot. One day he found a hardened criminal with a horrible face in a prison. His face displayed despair, greed, wickedness and sinfulness. By a special sanction, the prisoner was used as the model for painting the figure of Judas Iscariot. While the painting was in progress, the model showed great tension and uneasiness. When asked, he cried and confessed that a few years back he had posed as a model for the same painting - as the model for Jesus. The miserable man had left Jesus and the Church and turned to crime and sin, reaching a lamentable state of moral degeneration. His love changed to hatred, hope to despair and light to darkness! The painter is usually described as Leonardo da Vinci and the model is named Pietri Bandinelli in classical legends though historical evidence is lacking. But it is an excellent allegory revealing the spiritual degeneration in a person who rejects Jesus and turns to sinful ways. His fall is reflected even in his appearance, attitudes and attributes

IMPENDING ENDING

Damocles was one of the courtiers of King Dionysius II who ruled over the ancient kingdom of Syracuse (the Greek area of southern Italy) in the fourth century B.C. Damocles was much impressed by the immense wealth, luxurious life style, delicious food and palatial possessions of the king and used to remark that a king's life was the most fortunate experience on earth. The words of Damocles reached the king's ears. To teach him a lesson, the king arranged a banquet and gave Damocles a chance to adorn the royal throne. He was provided with attractive attendants, beautiful dancers, costly clothing, delicious drinks, delightful lighting, expensive decorations, exotic perfumes, fabulous food, fragrant flowers, fine furniture, melodious music, and luxurious surroundings.

Damocles felt that he was the most fortunate and the happiest man in the world. Suddenly he raised his eyes to the ceiling and was shocked to see a sharp sword suspended from the ceiling on a single horse hair, with its point almost touching his head. He was afraid that the fragile hair would snap at any moment and the heavy sword may fall on him and kill him. Terrified by the imminent danger, he could not enjoy any pleasure or luxury that surrounded him. He tearfully begged the king for relieving him from the present precarious predicament to return to his poor but peaceful and safer life. From this bitter experience, Damocles learned that happiness is fragile and that danger surrounds every powerful person. The phrase 'Damocles' sword' implies imminent peril and impending disaster.

'Death' is the Damocles' sword for all mortals.

Death often appears unexpectedly.

At every moment of life, we must be prepared and ready to meet and greet death as a friend. Life is short and all worldly riches and luxury have to be left behind when we die. They give only a temporary joy. Sinful indulgence in worldly pleasures may lead to everlasting agony in a hell of horror.

Death is the universal equalizer. Everyone is equal before death as death comes to all - great and small {Job 3: 13-19}. At his deathbed, Alexander the Great instructed his close associates to leave his hands hanging free on either side of the coffin during his royal funeral procession. That was to teach the world that he could carry nothing with him on his final journey. "Don't be upset when a man becomes rich, when his wealth grows even greater; he cannot take it with him when he dies; his wealth will not go with him to the grave.

Even if a man is satisfied with this life and is praised because he is successful, he will join all his ancestors in death, where the darkness lasts forever. A man's greatness cannot save him from death; he will still die like the animals" {Psalm 49:16-20}.

We fail to realize this truth till we reach the last moments in life. We waste a major share of our time, health and energy to amass fame, wealth and glory. In the parable of the rich fool, God says to the rich man, "You fool!

This very night you will have to give up your life: then who will get all these things you have kept for yourself?"{Luke 12:20}. Let us save our riches in heaven. Jesus taught us, "Provide for yourselves purses that don't wear out, and save your riches in heaven, where they will never decrease, because no thief can get to them and no moth can destroy them {Luke 12:33}.

A FATAL FLOOD

A river was in flood following heavy rain. The authorities warned the people staying near the river that a heavy flood was imminent and exhorted them to vacate their residences immediately and move to a safe camp, carrying only the most essential articles with them. First they sent a truck to carry the people. Most of them escaped in the truck.

One person was adamant that he would not follow them. He declared that he had a firm faith in God and was confident that God would save him.

The water from the overflowing river filled the lower areas and covered the roads. A rescue team was sent in a country boat in search of the remaining people to carry them to a safe place. The boatmen rowed along the roads, which were now submerged and announced their mission, inviting those trapped in their houses to escape in the boat.

The 'believer' still refused to enter the boat, repeating that he would continue to stay and pray till God came to save him. The boatmen left with the remaining people. The river burst its banks and flooded the valley. The overflowing water covered the houses one by one. The believer reached the terrace of his house and raising his hands to the sky, continued his prayer. The final rescue team surveyed the flood-hit area in a helicopter. They found the lone man on the terrace of his house and lowered a rope to him, shouting through a loudspeaker that he should hold on to the rope for being pulled into the helicopter and thus save himself. But the man was obstinate and adamant. He rejected their requests and refused to be saved. He stayed there, expecting God's direct intervention to save him. The last team left, abandoning the adamant believer.

The floods soon covered his house and he was drowned to death. Reaching heaven, he complained to God that He did not come to save his faithful servant in spite of his fervent prayers. God replied, "Son, I had come to you thrice - first in the truck, then in the boat and finally, in the helicopter. But you foolishly turned down my requests.

You wasted the three chances I gave you to save your life. "A person used to pray every day that he may win the first prize in a lottery. He was very sad as his prayer was not answered for a long time. Once he complained to God for not answering his only prayer. God told him in a dream, "Son, I am ready to grant your wish; but please purchase a lottery ticket first." That shows the prerequisite for an answer to our prayers: God wants our participation to perform a miracle in our life. When Jesus wanted to feed the thousands, He asked, "How much bread have you got? Go and see" {Mark 6:38}. He then accepted the boy's gift of five loaves and two fish and multiplied them miraculously.

ZEROES AND HEROES

A young lady was proudly narrating to the Vicar of her church, the qualities of her prospective bridegroom. He took a piece of paper and a pen and got ready to evaluate the person. As she excitedly enumerated each quality, he put a 'zero' mark on the paper, one after the other. She announced the attributes of the groom in alphabetical order: "He is affluent, beautiful, charming, dignified, educated and fashionable." She found that the Vicar has marked a zero as she mentioned each quality and was obviously not impressed by his action. Then she added, "He is also God-fearing."

Now the Vicar quickly marked a 'one' to the left of the six zeroes. The figure now read as: 1000000.

He said gladly, "Now there is a meaning to all the qualities you listed. Without God, we are zeroes.

With Him, we are heroes."

"The fear of the Lord is the beginning of wisdom" {Psalms 111:10}. "The fear of the Lord is the beginning of knowledge" {Proverbs 1:7}.

"Behold, the fear of the Lord is wisdom; and avoiding evil is understanding" {Job 28: 28}.

"For what this world considers to be wisdom is nonsense in God's sight"

{1 Corinthians 3: 19}.

DEAR DADDY

Two students in a college were close friends. One was the son of a rich merchant but his friend was very poor. The rich son used to spend money extravagantly and act recklessly. He wanted to make more money to live more lavishly.

He devised a plan to steal ornaments from a jewellery shop by night. He sought the assistance of the poor friend for the crime. They broke into the shop by night and stole some expensive jewellery.

The next day the police traced the culprits and they were held in custody. They were produced before the court of law and they were convicted of the crime by the court. The judge sentenced them to pay a heavy fine and decreed that they would be imprisoned if the fine was not paid forthwith. The rich man arrived in his expensive car with the required sum of money and easily paid the fine to release his son. The poor man had no money with him. There was nobody to help him. So he made a contract with the owner of a distant quarry that he would work for him in the quarry for a year. He received some money as an advance payment for his promised labour. With this money he could pay the fine and get his son released. But he had to shift to the quarry where he had to toil in the scorching summer to break the rocks and stones in the quarry and carry them to the trucks for transportation. His body became bruised by the laborious work and he got inflicted with several wounds. He shed a lot of blood and his body was scarred from the hard and dangerous work in the quarry. He had to stay in the clumsy temporary tents away from home for days together to continue his bonded labour. The two friends resumed their studies. One day the rich man's son invited his friend to join him in another operation of theft assuring that he had planned the operation meticulously and so they would not be traced this time. But the poor man's son declined the request remembering the hardships his loving father was suffering to compensate for the fine paid to save him from imprisonment. He told his rich friend, "My dear Daddy has shed his blood and bruised his body to save me. He is enduring this punishment for my sinful actions.

I will never commit another crime in my life."

Prophet Isaiah foretold the severe sufferings which Jesus endured to save us from the punishment that we deserved for our sins. "But he endured the suffering that should have been ours, the pain that we should have borne... But because of our sins he was wounded, beaten because of the evil we did. We are healed by the punishment he suffered, made whole by the blows he received" {Isaiah 53: 4,5}.

St. Peter teaches us, "Christ himself carried our sins in his body to the cross, so that we might die to sin and live for righteousness. It is by his wounds that you have been healed" {1 Peter 2: 24}.

Martin David Buxbaum (1912-1991), editor of Marriot's "Table Talk", tells parents that success in parenting is not measured by the expensive gifts and facilities you may provide to a child:

"You can use most any measure
When you are speaking of success.
You can measure it in fancy home,
Expensive car or dress.
But the measure of your real success
Is the one you cannot spend.
It's the way your kids describe you
When talking to a friend."

The family is the first and best institution founded by God. The letters in the word, FAMILY may be regarded as representing the first letters of the words in the statement, "Father And Mother In Love, Year-round"or the hearty remark of a loving little child, "Father and Mother! I Love You".

Parents should stand between their child and God- not as a separating wall but as a connecting link.

St. Paul advises us, "Put on all the armour that God gives you, so that you will be able to stand up against the Devil's evil tricks" {Ephesians 6: 11}.

St. Peter warns us, "Be alert, be on the watch! Your enemy, the Devil, roams round like a roaring lion, looking for someone to devour. Be firm in your faith and resist him, because you know that your fellow- believers in all the world are going through the same kind of sufferings" {1 Peter 5: 8, 9}.

A TREACHEROUS TRAP

There is a tale about an old trick used by some Africans to trap and capture wild monkeys.

They take a large nut with hard shell. A hole is made in the shell, just sufficient in size to let a monkey put its hand through it, but not big enough to let it withdraw its folded fist from the nut, when it is full of grabbed food. They put into the nut foods with fine smells such as orange peels, peanuts or small fruits. The nut is fastened firmly to a heavy rock or large tree and the trap is left in a place where monkeys visit regularly. Attracted by the smell of the food, an approaching monkey may eagerly introduce its hand inside the nut and grab a fistful of the food. As the hunters approach, the monkey tries its best to leave the nut but by instinct the monkey does not relax its grip on the food and so cannot escape from the trap. The frightened monkey may scream and try hard to pull out its hand but it tightens its grip as it lacks the sense to release its grasp. The monkey is then easily captured. Like the monkey in this story, we hold on to several silly pleasures and sinful situations. We have to be ready to leave our attachment to worthless worldly pleasures and affinity to material objects to gain true freedom and gather greater goals. Our desires impede our freedom. We should detach ourselves from these tempting desires. Otherwise we become slaves of Satan and sin. When we clasp worldly interests we fail to open our hands to receive the bliss of heavenly happiness. St. Ignatius Loyola used to repeat the following verse to St. Francis Xavier whenever they met in the campus of the University of Paris: "Will a person gain anything if he wins the whole world but loses his life?" {Matthew 16:26}. These words transformed St. Francis Xavier completely, gave him a new vision and mission and made him a great saint and missionary.

St. Paul teaches, "If you live according to your human nature, you are going to die; but if by the Spirit you put to death your sinful actions, you will live" {Romans 8: 13}.St. Paul declares, "But all those things that I might count as profit I now reckon as loss for Christ's sake. Not only those things; I reckon everything as complete loss for the sake of what is so much more valuable, the knowledge of Christ Jesus, my Lord. For His sake I have thrown everything away; I consider it all as mere refuse, so that I may gain Christ and be completely united with Him"{Philippians 3: 7-9}.

THE ROPE

The night fell heavy in the heights of the mountains and the man could not see anything. All was black. Zero visibility, and the moon and the stars were covered by the clouds. As he was climbing only a few feet away from the top of the mountain, he slipped and fell into the air, falling at great speed. He could only see black spots as he went down, and the terrible sensation of being sucked by gravity. He kept falling, and in the moments of great fear, it came to his mind all the good and bad episodes of his life. He was thinking now about how close death was getting, when all of a sudden he felt the rope tied to his waist pull him very hard. His body was hanging in the air. Only the rope was holding him and in that moment of stillness he had no other choice other than to scream: "Help me God." All of a sudden a deep voice coming from the sky answered, "What do you want me to do?"

"Save me God."

"Do you really think I can save you?"

"Of course I believe you can."

"Then cut the rope tied to your waist."

There was a moment of silence and the man decided to hold on to the rope with all his strength.

The rescue team tells that the next day a climber was

found dead and frozen, his body hanging from a rope. His hands holding tight to it. Only one foot away from the ground. And We? How attached we are to our rope will we let go??? Don't ever doubt about the words of God. We should never say that He has forgotten us or abandoned us.

CAN YOU SEE GOD?

A small boy once approached his slightly older sister with a question about God. "Susie, can anybody ever really see God?" he asked. Busy with other things, Susie curtly replied: "No, of course not silly. God is so far up in heaven that nobody can see him." Time passed, but his question still lingered so he approached his mom: "Mom, can anybody ever really see God?" "No, not really," she gently said. "God is a spirit and he dwells in our hearts, but we can never really see Him." Somewhat satisfied but still wondering, the youngster went on his way.

Not long afterwards, his saintly old grandfather took the little boy on a fishing trip. They were having a great time together. The sun was beginning to set with unusual splendor and the grandfather stared silently at the exquisite beauty unfolding before them. On seeing the face of his grandfather reflecting such deep peace and contentment, the little boy thought for a moment and finally spoke hesitatingly: "Granddad, I--I wasn't going to ask anybody else, but I wonder if you can tell me the answer to something I've been wondering about a long time. Can anybody - can anybody ever really see God?" The old man did not even turn his head. A long moment slipped by before he finally answered. "Son," he quietly said. "It's getting so I can't see anything else."

INSECT AND SPIDER

Once upon a time lived a spider in a cornfield. A big spider with a beautiful nest goes around between corn stems. It becomes fat by eating all the insects that trapped on its web. It really loved to live on that cornfield and plans to stay there forever.

One day, the spider catch a tiny insect on its web, and when this spider going to eat it, the insect said, “If you let me go, I will tell you one important thing that will save your life”. That spider stops for a moment and listen carefully. “You better go from this cornfield,” said this tiny insect, “Harvest time already here!”

The spider smiles and says, ”What this harvest time you talk about? I think you just make up a story”. But the tiny insects says, “Oh no, it’s true. The owner of this field will come soon to reap. All the corn stalk will be cut off and the corn will be gathered. You will be killed by a giant machine if you stay here."

The spider answers, "I do not believe in the harvest time or giant machine that will cut off the corn. How you may prove it?" The tiny insect continues, "Look at those corns. Look how those corns were planted in ordered lines. That proves that this field was designed by somebody brilliant".

The spider laugh and said, "This field grown by its own and has no relationship with a creator. Corns always grow like that". The insect explain more, "Oh no. This field owned by an owner who plants it, the harvest time will be here soon." The spider grinned and said; "I do not believe", and then it eat that insect. Few days later, the spider was laughing remembered the tiny insect's story. He thinks, "Harvest. What a stupid idea. I already here all my life and nobody is disturbing me. I already here when the plants just half meter tall from the ground, and will be here for the rest of my life, because there is nothing will changed on this field. Life is beautiful, and I will make it that way." The next day was a beautiful day on the cornfield. The sky was bright and there's no wind.

That noon, when the spider walks, he suddenly realizes there was a thick dust move on his way. It hears the sound of giant machine and told itself, "What is happening?" Luke 12:39 And this know, that if the good man of the house had known what hour the thief would come, he would have watched, and not have suffered his house to be broken through. Luke 12:40 Be ye therefore ready also: for the Son of man cometh at an hour when ye think not.

Matthew 13:36 Then Jesus sent the multitude away, and went into the house: and his disciples came unto him, saying, declare unto us the parable of the tares of the field.

Matthew 13:37 He answered and said unto them, He that soweth the good seed is the Son of man;

Matthew 13:38 The field is the world; the good seed are the children of the kingdom; but the tares are the children of the wicked [one];

Matthew 13:39 The enemy that sowed them is the devil; the harvest is the end of the world; and the reapers are the angels.

Matthew 13:40 As therefore the tares are gathered and burned in the fire; so shall it be in the end of this world.

Matthew 13:41 The Son of man shall send forth his angels, and they shall gather out of his kingdom all things that offend, and them which do iniquity;

Matthew 13:42 And shall cast them into a furnace of

fire: there shall be wailing and gnashing of teeth.

Matthew 13:43 Then shall the righteous shine forth as the sun in the kingdom of their Father. Who hath ears to hear, let him hear. The stair of life is full with wood shavings, but you will never realize it before you slipped down.

I ASKED GOD

I asked God to take away my pain.
God said, "No, It is not for me to take away, but for you to give it up".

I asked God to make my handicapped child whole.
God said, "No, her spirit was whole, her body was only temporary".

I asked God to grant me patience.
God said, "No, patience is a by-product of tribulations; it isn't granted, it is earned".

I asked God to give me happiness.
God said, "No, I give you blessings. Happiness is up to you". I asked God to spare me pain.
God said, "No, suffering draws you apart from worldly cares and brings you closer to me".

I asked God to make my spirit grow.
God said, "No, you must grow on your own, but I will prune you to make you fruitful".

I asked for all things that I might enjoy life.
God said, "No, I will give you life so that you may enjoy all things".

I ask God to help me love others, as much as he loves me.
God said, "... Ahhhh, finally you have the idea".

A MIRACLE

Like any good mother, when Karen found out that another baby was on the way, she did what she could to help her 3-year-old son, Michael, prepare for a new sibling. They found out that the new baby was going to be a girl, and day after day, night after night, Michael sang to his sister in Mommy's tummy. The pregnancy progressed normally for Karen, an active member of the Panther Creek United Methodist Church in Morristown, Tennessee. Then the labor pains came.

Every five minutes ... every minute. But complications arose during delivery. Hours of labour. Would a C-section be required? Finally, Michael's little sister was born. But she was in serious condition. With sirens howling in the night, the ambulance rushed the infant to the neonatal intensive care unit at St. Mary's Hospital, Knoxville,

Tennessee. The days inched by. The little girl became worse. The pediatric specialist told the parents to prepared for the worst. Karen and her husband contacted a local cemetery about a burial plot. They originally fixed up a special room in their home for the new baby - now they planned a funeral. Michael kept begging his parents to let him see his sister, "I want to sing to her," he said. Week two in intensive care. It looked as if a funeral would come before the week was over. Michael kept nagging about singing to his sister, but kids are not allowed in Intensive Care. Karen made up her mind. She decided to take Michael whether they like it or not. If he didn't see his sister now, he may never see her alive. She dressed him in an oversized scrub suit and marched him into ICU. He looked like a walking laundry basket, but the head nurse recognized him as a child and bellowed, "Get that kid out of here now! No children are allowed.

The mother in Karen rose up strong, and the usually

mild-mannered lady glared steel-eyed into the head nurse's face, her lips a firm line. "He is not leaving until he sings to his sister!" Karen towed Michael to his sister's bedside. He gazed at the tiny infant losing the battle to live. And he began to sing. In the pure hearted voice of a 3-year-old, Michael sang: "You are my sunshine, my only sunshine, you make me happy when skies are gray --- " Instantly the baby girl responded. The pulse rate became calm and steady. "Keep on singing, Michael." "You never know, dear, how much I love you, Please don't take my sunshine away---" Her strained breathing became smoother. "Keep on singing, Michael." "The other night, dear, as I lay sleeping, I dreamed I held you in my arms..." Michael's little sister relaxed as healing rest seemed to sweep over her. "Keep on singing, Michael." Tears conquered the face of the bossy head nurse. "You are my sunshine, my only sunshine. Please don't, take my sunshine away."

The next day--the very next day--the little girl was

well enough to go home! Woman's Day magazine called it "The Miracle of a Brother's Song." The medical staff just called it a miracle. Karen called it a miracle of God's love.

THE BEGGAR KING

Once there was a time, according to legend, when Ireland was ruled by a king who had no son. The king sent out his couriers to post notices in all the towns of his realm. The notices advised that every qualified young man should apply for an interview with the king as a possible successor to the throne. However, all such candidates must have these two qualifications:

They must (1) love God and (2) love their fellow human beings. The Young man about whom this legend centers saw a notice and reflected that he loved God and, also, his neighbors. One thing stopped him; he was so poor that he had no clothes that would be presentable in the sight of the king. Nor did he have the funds to buy provisions for the long journey to the castle. So the young man begged here, and borrowed there, finally managing to scrounge enough money for the appropriate clothes and the necessary supplies.

Properly attired and well-suited, the young man set out on his quest, and had almost completed the journey when he came upon a poor beggar by the side of the road. The beggar sat trembling, clad only in tattered rags. His extended arms pleaded for help. His weak voice croaked, "I'm hungry and cold. Please help me... please?" The young man was so moved by this beggar's need that he immediately stripped off his new clothes and put on the tattered threads of the beggar. Without a second thought he gave the beggar all his provision as well. Then, somewhat hesitantly, he continued his journey to the castle dressed in the rags of the beggar, lacking provisions for his return trek home.

Upon his arrival at the castle, a king's attendant showed him in to the great hall.

After a brief respite to clean off the journey's grime, he was finally admitted to the throne room of the king. The young man bowed low before his majesty. When he raised his eyes, he gaped in astonishment. "You... it's you! You're the beggar by the side of the road." "Yes," the king replied with a twinkle, "I was that beggar."

But...bu...bu... you are not really a beggar. You are the king for real. Well, then, why did you do this to me?" the young man stammered after gaining more of his composure.

“Because I had to find out if you genuinely love God and your fellow human beings," said the king.

"I knew that if I came to you as king, you would have been impressed by my gem-encrusted golden crown and my royal robes. You would have done anything I asked of you because of my regal character. But that way I would never have known what is truly in your heart. So I used a ruse. I came to you as a beggar with no claims on you except for the love in your hear. And I discovered that you sincerely do love God and your fellow human beings. You will be my successor," promised the king. "You will inherit my kingdom."

CHRISTMAS IS FOR LOVE

Christmas is for love. It is for joy, for giving and sharing, for laughter, for reuniting with family and friends, for tinsel and brightly decorated packages.

But mostly, Christmas is for love. I had not believed this until a small elf-like student with wide-eyed innocent eyes and soft rosy cheeks gave me a wondrous gift one Christmas.

Mark was an 11 year old orphan who lived with his aunt, a bitter middle aged woman greatly annoyed with the burden of caring for her dead sister's son. She never failed to remind young Mark, if it hadn't been for her generosity, he would be a vagrant, homeless waif. Still, with all the scolding and chilliness at home, he was a sweet and gentle child.

I had not noticed Mark particularly until he began staying after class each day (at the risk of arousing his aunt's anger, I later found) to help me straighten up the room.

We did this quietly and comfortably, not speaking much, but enjoying the solitude of that hour of the day. When we did talk, Mark spoke mostly of his mother. Though he was quite small when she died, he remembered a kind, gentle, loving woman, who always spent much time with him.

As Christmas drew near however, Mark failed to stay after school each day. I looked forward to his coming, and when the days passed and he continued to scamper hurriedly from the room after class, I stopped him one afternoon and asked why he no longer helped me in the room. I told him how I had missed him, and his large gray eyes lit up eagerly as he replied, "Did you really miss me?"

I explained how he had been my best helper. "I was making you a surprise," he whispered confidentially. "It's for Christmas." With that, he became embarrassed and dashed from the room. He didn't stay after school any more after that.

Finally came the last school day before Christmas. Mark crept slowly into the room late that afternoon with his hands concealing something behind his back. "I have your present," he said timidly when I looked up. "I hope you like it." He held out his hands, and there lying in his small palms was a tiny wooden box. "It's beautiful, Mark. Is there something in it?" I asked opening the top to look inside. ""Oh you can't see what's in it," He replied, "and you can't touch it, or taste it or feel it, but mother always said it makes you feel good all the time, warm on cold nights, and safe when you're all alone."I gazed into the empty box. "What is it Mark," I asked gently, "that will make me feel so good?" "It's love," he whispered softly, "and mother always said it's best when you give it away." And he turned and quietly left the room. So now I keep a small box crudely made of scraps of wood on the piano in my living room and only smile as inquiring friends raise quizzical eyebrows when I explain to them that there is love in it. Yes, Christmas is for gaiety, mirth and song, for good and wondrous gifts. But mostly, Christmas is for love.

A CHILD'S TEN COMMANDMENTS TO PARENTS

1. My hands are small. Please don't expect perfection whenever I make a bed, draw a picture or throw a ball. My legs are short. Please slow down so that I can keep up with you.

2. My eyes have not seen the world as yours have.

Please let me explore safely. Don't restrict me unnecessarily.

3. Housework will always be there. I'm only little for such a short time. Please take time to explain things to me about this wonderful world, and do so willingly.

4. My feelings are tender. Please be sensitive to my needs. Don't nag me all day long. (You wouldn't

want to be nagged for your inquisitiveness.) Treat me as you would like to be treated.

5. I am a special gift from God. Please treasure me, holding me accountable for my actions, giving me guidelines to live by and disciplining me in a loving manner.

6. I need your encouragement and your praise to grow. Please go easy on the criticism. Remember,

you can criticize the things I do without criticizing me.

7. Please give me the freedom to make decisions concerning myself. Permit me to fail so that I can learn from my mistakes.

Then someday, I'll be prepared to make the kind of decisions life requires of me.

8. Please don't do things over for me. Somehow that makes me feel that my efforts didn't quite measure up to your expectations. I know it's hard, but please don't try to compare me with my brother or my sister.

9. Please don't be afraid to leave for a weekend together. Kids need vacations from parents, just as parents need vacations from kids. Besides, it's a great way to show us kids that your marriage is very special.

10. Please take me to worship regularly, setting a good example for me to follow.

THE LETTER

Ruth went to her mail box and there was only one letter. She picked it up and looked at it before opening, but then she looked at the envelope again. There was no stamp, no postmark, only her name and address.

She read the letter:

Dear Ruth,

I'm going to be in your neighborhood Saturday afternoon and I'd like to stop by for a visit.

Love Always, Jesus

Her hands were shaking as she placed the letter on the table. "Why would the Lord want to visit me?

I'm nobody special. I don't have anything to offer." With that thought, Ruth remembered her empty kitchen cabinets. "Oh my goodness, I really don't have anything to offer. I'll have to run down to the store and buy something for dinner." She reached for her purse and counted out its contents. Five dollars and forty cents.

"Well, I can get some bread and cold cuts, at least." She threw on her coat and hurried out the door. A loaf of French bread, a half-pound of sliced turkey, and a carton of milk...leaving Ruth with a grand total of twelve cents to last her until Monday.

Nonetheless, she felt good as she headed home, her meager offerings tucked under her arm. "Hey lady, can you help us, lady?" Ruth had been so absorbed in her dinner plans; she hadn't even noticed two figures huddled in the alleyway. A man and a woman, both of them dressed in little more than rags.

"Look lady, I ain't got a job, ya know, and my wife and I have been living out here on the street, and, well, now it's getting cold and we're getting kinda hungry and, well, if you could help us, lady, we'd really appreciate it." Ruth looked at them both.

They were dirty, they smelled bad and, frankly, she was certain that they could get some kind of work if they really wanted to. "Sir, I'd like to help you, but I'm a poor woman myself. All I have is a few cold cuts and some bread, and I'm having an important guest for dinner tonight and I was planning on serving that to Him."

"Yeah, well, okay lady, I understand. Thanks anyway." The man put his arm around the woman's shoulders, turned and headed back into the alley.

As she watched them leave, Ruth felt a familiar twinge in her heart. "Sir, wait!" The couple stopped and turned as she ran down the alley after them. "Look, why don't you take this food. I'll figure out something else to serve my guest." She handed the man her grocery bag. "Thank you lady. Thank you very much!" "Yes, thank you!" It was the man's wife, and Ruth could see now that she was shivering.

"You know, I've got another coat at home. Here, why don't you take this one." Ruth unbuttoned her jacket and slipped it over the woman's shoulders. Then smiling, she turned and walked back to the street...without her coat and with nothing to serve her guest. Thank you lady! Thank you very much!"

Ruth was chilled by the time she reached her front door, and worried too.

The Lord was coming to visit and she didn't have anything to offer Him. She fumbled through her purse for the door key. But as she did, she noticed another envelope in her mailbox. "That's odd. The mailman doesn't usually come twice in one day." She took the envelope out of the box and opened it.

ENLIGHTMENT

Buddha reached the gate of heaven. Of course, the people there were waiting. They opened the door, they welcomed him, but he turned his back towards the door looked at the world -- millions of souls on the same path, struggling, in misery, in anguish, striving to reach this gate of heaven and bliss.

The doorkeeper said, "Come in, please. We have been waiting for you"

Buddha said, "How can I come when others have not reached? It doesn't seem to be the right time. How can I enter when the whole has not yet entered? I will have to wait. It is just as if my hands has reached into the door and my feet have not reached yet. I will have to wait. Just the hand cannot enter alone."

A GIFT FROM GOD

One day, when I was a freshman in high school, I saw a kid from my class was walking home from school. His name was Kyle. It looked like he was carrying all of his books. I thought to myself, "Why would anyone bring home all his books on a Friday? He must really be a nerd." I had quite a weekend planned (parties and a football game with my friends' tomorrow afternoon), so I shrugged my shoulders and went on. As I was walking, I saw a bunch of kids running toward him. They ran at him, knocking all his books out of his arms and tripping him so he landed in the dirt. His glasses went flying, and I saw them land in the grass about ten feet from him. He looked up and I saw this terrible sadness in his eyes. My heart went out to him. So, I jogged over to him and as he crawled around looking for his glasses, and I saw a tear in his eye. As I handed him his glasses, I said, "Those guys are jerks. They really should get lives." He looked at me and said, "Hey thanks!" There was a big smile on his face.

It was one of those smiles that showed real gratitude. I helped him pick up his books, and asked him where he lived. As it turned out, he lived near me, so I asked him why I had never seen him before. He said he had gone to private school before now. I would have never hung out with a private school kid before.

We talked all the way home, and I carried his books. He turned out to be a pretty cool kid. I asked him if he wanted to play football on Saturday with me and my friends. He said yes.

We hung all weekend and the more I got to know Kyle, the more I liked him. And my friends thought the same of him. Monday morning came, and there was Kyle with the huge stack of books again.

I stopped him and said, "Darn boy, you are gonna

really build some serious muscles with this pile of books everyday!" He just laughed and handed me half the books. Over the next four years, Kyle and I became best friends. When we were seniors, we began to think about college. Kyle decided on Georgetown, and I was going to Duke. I knew that we would always be friends, that the miles would never be a problem. He was going to be a doctor, and I was going for business on a football scholarship. Kyle was valedictorian of our class. I teased him all the time about being a nerd. He had to prepare a speech for graduation. I was so glad it wasn't me having to get up there and speak.

Graduation day, I saw Kyle. He looked great. He was one of those guys that really found himself during high school. He filled out and actually looked good in glasses. He had more dates than me and all the girls loved him! Boy, sometimes I was jealous. Today was one of those days. I could see that he was nervous about his speech. So, I smacked him on the back and said, "Hey, big guy, you'll be great!" He looked at me with one of those looks (the really grateful one) and smiled. "Thanks," he said.

As he started his speech, he cleared his throat, and began. "Graduation is a time to thank those who helped you make it through those tough years. Your parents, your teachers, your siblings, maybe a coach ... , but mostly your friends. I am here to tell all of you that being a friend to someone is the best gift you can give them. I am going to tell you a story."

I just looked at my friend with disbelief as he told the story of the first day we met. He had planned to kill himself over the weekend. He talked of how he had cleaned out his locker so his mom wouldn't have to do it later and was carrying his stuff home.

He looked hard at me and gave me a little smile. "Thankfully, I was saved. My friend saved me from doing the unspeakable."

I heard the gasp go through the crowd as this handsome, popular boy told us all about his weakest moment. I saw his mom and dad looking at me and smiling that same grateful smile. Not until that moment did I realize its depth.

Never underestimate the power of your actions. With one small gesture you can change a person's life. For better or for worse. God puts us all in each other's lives to impact one another in some way. Look for God in others.

Each day is a gift from God! Don't forget to say, "Thank you!"

GOD'S POWER IN ACTION

God has a way of allowing us to be in the right place at the right time. I was walking down a dimly lit street late one evening when I heard muffled screams coming from behind a clump of bushes. Alarmed, I slowed down to listen, and panicked when I realized that what I was hearing were the unmistakable sounds of a struggle: heavy grunting, frantic scuffling, and tearing of fabric.

Only yards from where I stood, a woman was being attacked. Should I get involved? I was frightened for my own safety, and cursed myself for having suddenly decided to take a new route home that night. What if I became another statistic? Shouldn't I just run to the nearest phone and call the police?

Although it seemed an eternity, the deliberations in my head had taken only seconds, but already the girl's cries were growing weaker.

I knew I had to act fast. How could I walk away from this? No, I finally resolved, I could not turn my back on the fate of this unknown woman, even if it meant risking my own life.

I am not a brave man, nor am I athletic. I don't know where I found the moral courage and physical strength -- but once I had finally resolved to help the girl, I became strangely transformed. I ran behind the bushes and pulled the assailant off the woman. Grappling, we fell to the ground, where we wrestled for a few minutes until the attacker jumped up and escaped. Panting hard, I scrambled upright and approached the girl, who was crouched behind a tree, sobbing. In the darkness, I could barely see her outline, but I could certainly sense her trembling shock. Not wanting to frighten her further, I at first spoke to her from a distance.

"It's okay," I said soothingly. "The man ran away. You're safe now." There was a long pause and then I heard the words, uttered in wonder, in amazement. "Dad, is that you?" And then, from behind the tree, out stepped my youngest daughter, Katherine.

CHRISTMAS BOOTS AND SHOES

Bobby was getting cold sitting out in his back yard in the snow. Bobby didn't wear boots; he didn't like them and anyway he didn't own any. The thin sneakers he wore had a few holes in them and they did a poor job of keeping out the cold.

Bobby had been in his backyard for about an hour already. And, try as he might, he could not come up with an idea for his mother's Christmas gift. He shook his head as he thought, "This is useless, even if I do come up with an idea, and I don't have any money to spend."Ever since his father had passed away three years ago, the family of five had struggled. It wasn't because his mother didn't care, or try, there just never seemed to be enough. She worked nights at the hospital, but the small wage that she was earning could only be stretched so far.

What the family lacked in money and material things, they more than made up for in love and family unity. Bobby had two older and one younger sister, who ran the household in their mother's absence. All three of his sisters had already made beautiful gifts for their mother.

Somehow it just wasn't fair. Here it was Christmas Eve already, and he had nothing.

Wiping a tear from his eye, Bobby kicked the snow

and started to walk down to the street where the shops and stores were. It wasn't easy being six without a father, especially when he needed a man to talk to. Bobby walked from shop to shop, looking into each decorated window. Everything seemed so beautiful and so out of reach. It was starting to get dark and Bobby reluctantly turned to walk home when suddenly his eyes caught the glimmer of the setting sun's rays reflecting off of something along the curb. He reached down and discovered a shiny dime. Never before has anyone felt so wealthy as Bobby felt at that moment. As he held his new found treasure, a warmth spread throughout his entire body and he walked into the first store he saw. His excitement quickly turned cold when salesperson after salesperson told him that he could not buy anything with only a dime.

He saw a flower shop and went inside to wait in line. When the shop owner asked if he could help him, Bobby presented the dime and asked if he could buy one flower for his mother's Christmas gift. The shop owner looked at Bobby and his ten cent offering. Then he put his hand on Bobby's shoulder and said to him, "You just wait here and I'll see what I can do for you."

As Bobby waited, he looked at the beautiful flowers and even though he was a boy, he could see why mothers and girls liked flowers.

The sound of the door closing as the last customer left, jolted Bobby back to reality. All alone in the shop, Bobby began to feel alone and afraid.

Suddenly the shop owner came out and moved to the counter. There, before Bobby's eyes, lay twelve long stem, red roses, with leaves of green and tiny white flowers all tied together with a big silver bow. Bobby's heart sank as the owner picked them up and placed them gently into a long white box.

"That will be ten cents young man." the shop owner said reaching out his hand for the dime. Slowly, Bobby moved his hand to give the man his dime.

Could this be true?

No one else would give him a thing for his dime!

Sensing the boy's reluctance, the shop owner added, "I just happened to have some roses on sale for ten cents a dozen. Would you like them?"

This time Bobby did not hesitate, and when the man placed the long box into his hands, he knew it was true. Walking out the door that the owner was holding for Bobby, he heard the shop keeper say, "Merry Christmas, son." As he returned inside, the shop keepers' wife walked out. "Who were you talking to back there and where are the roses you were fixing?"

Staring out the window, and blinking the tears from his own eyes, he replied, "A strange thing happened to me this morning. While I was setting up things to open the shop, I thought I heard a voice telling me to set aside a dozen of my best roses for a special gift. I wasn't sure at the time whether I had lost my mind or what, but I set them aside anyway.

Then just a few minutes ago, a little boy came into the shop and wanted to buy a flower for his mother with one small dime. "When I looked at him, I saw myself, many years ago. I too, was a poor boy with nothing to buy my mother a Christmas gift.
A bearded man, whom I never knew, stopped me on the street and told me that he wanted to give me ten dollars. "When I saw that little boy tonight, I knew who that voice was, and I put together a dozen of my very best roses." The shop owner and his wife hugged each other tightly, and as they stepped out into the bitter cold air, they somehow didn't feel cold at all.

A WHIP IN HIS HAND

Compassion is not having a bleeding heart full of sympathy for others -- compassion is such a depth of love that one is willing to do whatever it takes to bring awareness to a situation. Let me remind you of a situation that happened in Jesus' life. He took a whip and entered the great temple of Jerusalem. A whip in the hand of Jesus? Yes, Jesus can handle a whip, no problems; the whip cannot overpower him. He remains alert, his consciousness is such.

The great temple of Jerusalem had become a place of robbers. A subtle robbery was going on.

There were money changers inside the temple, and they were exploiting the whole country.

Jesus entered their temple alone and upturned their boards -- the boards of the money changers -- threw their money and created such turmoil that the moneychangers escaped outside the temple. They were many and Jesus was alone, but he was in such a fury, in such a fire! Now, how do we explain this? Jesus is the dove, a man of peace.

How could he take a whip in his hands? How could he be so angry, so enraged, that he upturned the boards of the moneychangers and threw the moneychangers out of the temple? And his energy must have been in a storm.

They could not face him. The priests and the business people and the moneychangers all escaped, shouting, "This man has gone mad!"

Jesus is absolutely innocent! He is not violent. He is not destructive. It is his compassion.

It is his love. The whip in his hands is the whip in the hands of love.

A PENNY

Several years ago, a friend of mine and her husband were invited to spend the weekend at the husband's employer's home. My friend, Arlene, was nervous about the weekend. The boss was very wealthy, with a fine home on the waterway, and cars costing more than her house. The first day and evening went well, and Arlene was delighted to have this rare glimpse into how the very wealthy live. The husband's employer was quite generous as a host, and took them to the finest restaurants. Arlene knew she would never have the opportunity to indulge in this kind of extravagance again, so was enjoying herself immensely. As the three of them were about to enter an exclusive restaurant that evening, the boss was walking slightly ahead of Arlene and her husband. He stopped suddenly, looking down on the pavement for a long, silent moment. Arlene wondered if she was supposed to pass him. There was nothing on the ground except a single darkened penny that someone had dropped, and a few cigarette butts. Still silent, the man reached down and picked up the penny.

He held it up and smiled, then put it in his pocket as if he had found a great treasure. How absurd! What need did this man have for a single penny? Why would he even take the time to stop and pick it up? Throughout dinner, the entire scene nagged at her. Finally, she could stand it no longer.

She causally mentioned that her daughter once had a

coin collection, and asked if the penny he had found had been of some value. A smile crept across the man's face as he reached into his pocket for the penny and held it out for her to see. She had seen many pennies before!

What was the point of this?

"Look at it." He said. "Read what it says."

She read the words "United States of America."

"No, not that; read further."

"One cent?"

"No, keep reading."

"In God we Trust?"

"Yes!""And?"

"And if I trust in God, the name of God is holy, even on a coin. Whenever I find a coin I see that inscription. It is written on every single United States coin, but we never seem to notice it! God drops a message right in front of me telling me to trust Him? Who am I to pass it by? When I see a coin, I pray, I stop to see if my trust IS in God at that moment. I pick the coin up as a response to God; that I do trust in Him.

For a short time, at least, I cherish it as if it were gold. I think it is God's way of starting a conversation with me. Lucky for me, God is patient and pennies are plentiful!

When I was out shopping today, I found a penny on the sidewalk. I stopped and picked it up, and realized that I had been worrying and fretting in my mind about things I cannot change. I read the words, "In God We Trust," and had to laugh. Yes, God, I get the message.

It seems that I have been finding an inordinate number of pennies in the last few months, but then, pennies are plentiful!

And, God is patient...

Have a blessed day!!

The best mathematical equation I have ever seen:

1 cross + 3 nails -------- 4 given

A PRAYER OF A DYING CHILD

I woke up one morning and I was 17,
I knew the day had come
The day I prove to everyone how cool I was
The day I accepted death as my destiny
Little did I know I would regret that day
And my family who kept me alive for 17 years
Would be cursed by me for years of never ending pain
Without thinking I lit the cigarette
I knew it had to be done before the day was over
I coughed a little but I was fine
Now as I lay in bed coughing and choking
My family is beside me

My parents and my sister
I whisper in my sister's ear

"Please don't do what I did"

She just nodded her head in silence

Now as my angel holds me in his arms

I know it's time for me to go

I close my eyes and kiss him one last time

It's funny how we resent those who try to help us when we're alive

And how we beg them to save us when we're about to die

All this because of one silly cigarette

All this because someone was dumb enough to say that Smoking is cool.

ARE YOU BLESSED?

If you woke up this morning with more health than illness..........you are more blessed than the million who will not survive this week.

If you have never experienced the danger of battle,

the loneliness of imprisonment, the agony of torture, or the pangs of starvation.......you are ahead of 500 million people in the world.

If you have food in the refrigerator, clothes on your back, a roof overhead and a place to sleep...you are richer than 75% of this world.

If you have money in the bank, in your wallet, and spare change in a dish someplace....... you are among the top 8% of the world's wealthy.

If your parents are still alive and still married........you are very rare, even in the United States.

If you hold up your head with a smile on your face and are truly thankful.....you are blessed because the majority can, but most do not.

If you prayed yesterday and today........you are in the minority because you believe God does hear and answer prayers.

If you can read now, you are more blessed than over

two billion people in the world that cannot read at all.

THEY CRUCIFIED HIM

A medical doctor provides a physical description:

The cross is placed on the ground and the exhausted man is quickly thrown backwards with his shoulders against the wood. The legionnaire feels for the depression at the front of the wrist. He drives a heavy, square wrought-iron nail through the wrist deep into the wood. Quickly he moves to the other side and repeats the action, being careful not to pull the arms too tightly, but to allow some flex and movement. The cross is then lifted into place. The left foot is pressed backward against the right foot, and with both feet extended, toes down, a nail is driven through the arch of each, leaving the knees flexed. The victim is now crucified.

As he slowly sags down with more weight on the nails in the wrists, excruciating fiery pain shoots along the fingers and up the arms to explode in the brain -- the nails in the wrists are putting pressure on the median nerves. As he pushes himself upward to avoid this stretching torment, he places the full weight on the nail through his feet. Again he feels the searing agony of the nail tearing through the nerves between the bones of his feet.

As the arms fatigue, cramps sweep through his muscles, knotting them deep relentless, and throbbing pain. With these cramps comes the inability to push himself upward to breathe. Air can be drawn into the lungs but not exhaled. He fights to raise himself in order to get even one small breath.

Finally, carbon dioxide builds up in the lungs and in the blood stream, and the cramps partially subsided. Spasmodically, he is able to push himself upward to exhale and bring in life-giving oxygen.

Hours of limitless pain, cycles of twisting, joint-renting cramps, intermittent partial asphyxiation, searing pain as tissue is torn from his lacerated back as he moves up and down against rough timber. Then another agony begins: a deep, crushing pain deep in the chest as the pericardium slowly fills with serum and begins to compress the heart. It is now almost over. The loss of tissue fluids has reached a critical level. The compressed heart is struggling to pump heavy, thick, sluggish blood into the tissues. The tortured lungs are making frantic effort to gasp in small gulps of air. He can feel the chill of death creeping through his tissues.

Finally, he allows his body to die. All this the Bible

records with the simple words, "and they crucified Him" -- Mark 15:24

DON'T FORGET TO SMILE

A little girl walked to and from school daily. Though the weather that morning was questionable and clouds were forming, she made her daily trek to the elementary school. As the afternoon progressed, the winds whipped up, along with thunder and lightning. The mother of the little girl felt concerned that her daughter would be frightened as she walked home from school and she herself feared that the electrical storm might harm her child. Following the roar of thunder, lightning, like a flaming sword, would cut through the sky. Full of concern, the mother quickly got into her car and drove along the route to her child's school. As she did so, she saw her little girl walking along, but at each flash of lightning, the child would stop, look up and smile. Another and another were to follow quickly and with each the little girl would look at the streak of light and smile. When the mother's car drove up beside the child she lowered the window and called to her. "What are you doing? Why do you keep stopping?" The child answered, "I am trying to look pretty, God keeps taking my picture. "May God bless you today as you face the storms that come your way.

IS PACKAGING IMPORTANT

A young man was getting ready to graduate from college. For many months he had admired a beautiful sports car in a dealer's showroom, and knowing his father could well afford it, he told him that was all he wanted.

As Graduation Day approached, the young man awaited signs that his father had purchased the car. Finally, on the morning of his graduation, his father called him into his private study. His father told him how proud he was to have such a fine son, and told him how much he loved him. He handed his son a beautiful wrapped gift box.

Curious, but somewhat disappointed, the young man opened the box and found a lovely, leather-bound Bible, with the young man's name embossed in gold. Angrily, he raised his voice to his father and said, "With all your money you give me a Bible?" He then stormed out of the house, leaving the Bible.

Many years passed and the young man was very successful in business. He had a beautiful home and a wonderful family, but realizing his father was very old, he thought perhaps he should go to see him. He had not seen him since that graduation day. Before he could make the arrangements, he received a telegram telling him his father had passed away, and willed all of his possessions to his son. He needed to come home immediately and take care of things.

When he arrived at his father's house, sudden

sadness and regret filled his heart.

He began to search through his father's important papers and saw the still new Bible, just as he had left it years ago. With tears, he opened the Bible and began to turn the pages. As he was reading, a car key dropped from the back of the Bible. It had a tag with the dealer's name, the same dealer who had the sports car he had desired. On the tag was the date of his graduation, and the words... "PAID IN FULL".

How many times do we miss blessings because they are not packaged as we expected?

I trust you enjoyed this. Pass it on to others. Do not spoil what you have by desiring what you have not; but remember that what you now have was once among the things you only hoped for.

IS YOUR HUT BURNING?

The only survivor of a shipwreck was washed up on a small, uninhabited island. He prayed feverishly for God to rescue him, and every day he scanned the horizon for help, but none seemed forthcoming .Exhausted, he eventually managed to build a little hut out of driftwood to protect Him from the elements, and to store his few possessions. Then one day, after scavenging for food, he arrived home to find his little hut in flames, the smoke rolling up to the sky. The worst had happened; everything was lost. He was stunned with grief and anger. "God, how could you do this to me!" he cried. Early the next day, however, he was awakened by the sound of a ship that was approaching the island. It had come to rescue him. "How did you know I was here?" asked the weary man of his rescuers. "We saw your smoke signal," they replied.

It is easy to get discouraged when things are going bad. But we shouldn't lose heart, because God is at work in our lives, even in the midst of pain and suffering. Remember, next time your little hut is burning to the ground-it just may be a smoke signal that summons the grace of God.

For all the negative things we have to say to ourselves, God has a positive answer for it.

You say: "It's impossible"
God says: All things are possible (Luke 18:27)

You say: "I'm too tired"
God says: I will give you rest (Matthew 11:28-30)

You say: "Nobody really loves me"
God says: I love you (John 3:16 & John 13:34)

You say: "I can't go on"

God says: My grace is sufficient (II Corinthians 12:9& Psalm 91:15)

You say: "I can't figure things out"

God says: I will direct your steps (Proverbs 3:5-6)

You say: "I can't do it"

God says: You can do all things (Philippians 4:13)

You say: "I'm not able"

God says: I am able (II Corinthians 9:8)

You say: "It's not worth it"

God says: It will be worth it (Roman 8:28)

You say: "I can't forgive myself"

God says: I FORGIVE YOU (I John 1:9 & Romans 8:1)

You say: "I can't manage"

God says: I will supply all your needs (Philippians 4:19)

You say: "I'm afraid"
God says: I have not given you a spirit of fear (II Timothy 1:7)

You say: "I'm always worried and frustrated"
God says: Cast all your cares on ME (I Peter 5:7)

You say: "I don't have enough faith"
God says: I've given everyone a measure of faith (Romans 12:3)

You say: "I'm not smart enough"
God says: I give you wisdom (I Corinthians 1:30)

You say: "I feel all alone"
God says: I will never leave you or forsake you (Hebrews 13:5)

GOD WORKS IN MYSTERIOUS WAYS

It was an unusually cold day for the month of May. Spring had arrived and everything was alive with colour. But a cold front from the North had brought winter's chill back to Indiana. I sat, with two friends, in the picture window of a quaint restaurant just off the corner of the towns-square. The food and the company were both especially good that day. As we talked, my attention was drawn outside, across the street. There, walking into town, was a man who appeared to be carrying all his worldly goods on his back. He was carrying, a well-worn sign that read, and “I will work for food."My heart sank. I brought him to the attention of my friends and noticed that others around us had stopped eating to focus on him. Heads moved in a mixture of sadness and disbelief. We continued with our meal, but his image lingered in my mind. We finished our meal and went our separate ways.I had errands to do and quickly set out to accomplish them. I glanced toward the town square, looking somewhat half-heartedly for the strange visitor. I was fearful, knowing that seeing him again would call some response. I drove through town and saw nothing of him. I made some purchases at a store and got back in my car.Deep within me, the Spirit of God kept speaking to me: "Don't go back to the office until you've at least driven once more around the square." And so, with some hesitancy, I headed back into town. As I turned the square's third corner. I saw him. He was standing on the steps of the storefront church, going through his sack. I stopped and looked, feeling both compelled to speak to him, yet wanting to drive on.The empty parking space on the corner seemed to be a sign from God: an invitation to park. I pulled in, got out and approached the town's newest visitor. "Looking for the pastor?"

I asked. "Not really," he replied, "just resting."

"Have you eaten today?" "Oh, I ate something early this morning."

"Would you like to have lunch with me?"

"Do you have some work I could do for you?"

"No work," I replied. "I commute here to work from the city, but I would like to take you to lunch."

"Sure," he replied with a smile.

As he began to gather his things. I asked some surface questions. "Where are you headed?"

"St. Louis."

"Where you from?" "Oh, all over; mostly Florida."

"How long you been walking?"

"Fourteen years," came the reply.

I knew I had met someone unusual. We sat across from each other in the same restaurant I had left earlier. His face was weathered slightly beyond his 38 years. His eyes were dark yet clear, and he spoke with an eloquence and articulation that was startling. He removed his jacket to reveal a bright red T-shirt that said, "Jesus is The Never Ending Story."

Then Daniel's story began to unfold. He had seen rough times early in life. He'd made some wrong choices and reaped the consequences. Fourteen years earlier, while backpacking across the country, he had stopped on the beach in Daytona.

He tried to hire on with some men who were putting up a large tent and some equipment. A concert, he thought. He was hired, but the tent would not house a concert but revival services, and in those services he saw life more clearly.

He gave his life over to God. "Nothing's been the same since," he said, "I felt the Lord telling me to keep walking, and so I did, some 14 years now."

"Ever think of stopping?" I asked.

"Oh, once in a while, when it seems to get the best of me.

But God has given me this calling.
I give out Bibles.

That's what's in my sack. I work to buy food and Bibles, and I give them out when His Spirit leads."

I sat amazed. My homeless friend was not homeless. He was on a mission and lived this way by choice. The question burned inside for a moment and then

I asked: "What's it like?"

"What?"

"To walk into a town carrying all your things on your back and to show your sign?"

"Oh, it was humiliating at first. People would stare and make comments.

Once someone tossed a piece of half-eaten bread and made a gesture that certainly didn't make me feel welcome. But then it became humbling to realize that God was using me to touch lives and change people's concepts of other folks like me."

My concept was changing, too. We finished our dessert and gathered his things. Just outside the door, he paused. He turned to me and said, "Come, Ye blessed of my Father, and inherit the kingdom I've prepared for you. For when I was hungry you gave me food, when I was thirsty you gave me drink, a stranger and you took me in."

I felt as if we were on holy ground.

"Could you use another Bible?" I asked.

He said he preferred a certain translation. It travelled well and was not too heavy. It was also his personal favourite. "I've read through it 14 times," he said. "I'm not sure we've got one of those, but let's stop by our church and see."

I was able to find my new friend a Bible that would do well, and he seemed very grateful.

"Where you headed from here?"

"Well, I found this little map on the back of this amusement park coupon."

"Are you hoping to hire on there for a while?"

"No, I just figure I should go there. I figure someone under that star right there needs a Bible, so that's where I'm going next." He smiled, and the warmth of his spirit radiated the sincerity of his mission.

I drove him back to the town-square where we'd met two hours earlier, and as we drove, it started raining. We parked and unloaded his things.

Would you sign my autograph book?" he asked.

"I like to keep messages from folks I meet."

I wrote in his little book that his commitment to his calling had touched my life. I encouraged him to stay strong. And I left him with a verse of scripture from Jeremiah, "I know the plans I have for you," declared the Lord, "plans to prosper you and not to harm you. Plans to give you a future and a hope."

"Thanks, man," he said. "I know we just met and we're really just strangers, but I love you."

"I know," I said, "I love you, too."

"The Lord is good."

"Yes, He is. How long has it been since someone hugged you?" I asked.

"A long time," he replied.

And so on the busy street corner in the drizzling rain, my new friend and I embraced, and I felt deep inside that I had been changed. He put his things on his back, smiled his winning smile and said, "See you in the New Jerusalem."

"I'll be there!" was my reply.

He began his journey again. He headed away with his sign dangling from his bed roll and pack of Bibles. He stopped, turned and said, "When you see something that makes you think of me, will you pray for me?"

"You bet," I shouted back, "God bless."

"God bless." And that was the last I saw of him. Late that evening as I left my office, the wind blew strong. The cold front had settled hard upon the town. I bundled up and hurried to my car. As I sat back and reached for the emergency brake, I saw them... a pair of well-worn brown work gloves neatly laid over the length of the handle. I picked them up and thought of my friend and wondered if his hands would stay warm that night without them. I remembered his words: "If you see something that makes you think of me, will you pray for me?"Today his gloves lie on my desk in my office. They help me to see the world and its people in a new way, and they help me remember those two hours with my unique friend and to pray for his ministry.

"See you in the New Jerusalem," he said.

Yes, Daniel, I know I will.

CAN ANYONE SEE GOD

A small boy once approached his slightly older sister with a question about God.

"Susie, can anybody ever really see God?" he asked. Busy with other things, Susie curtly replied: "No, of course not, silly. God is so far up in heaven that nobody can see him."

Time passed, but his question still lingered, so he

approached his mother: "Mom, can anybody ever really see God?" "No, not really," she gently said. "God is a spirit and he dwells in our hearts, but we can never really see him."

Somewhat satisfied but still wondering, the youngster went on his way. Not long afterwards, his saintly old grandfather took the little boy on a fishing trip. They were having a great time together -- it had been an ideal day. The sun was beginning to set with unusual splendour as the day ended.

The old man stopped fishing and turned his full attention to the exquisite beauty unfolding before him. On seeing the face of his grandfather reflecting such deep peace and contentment as he gazed into the magnificent ever-changing sunset, the little boy thought for a moment and finally spoke hesitatingly:

"Granddad, I - I wasn't going to ask anybody else, but I wonder if you can tell me the answer to something I've been wondering about a long time. Can anybody, can anybody ever really see God?"

The old man did not even turn his head. A long moment slipped by before he finally answered. "Son," he quietly said. "It's getting so I can't see anything else."

"The heavens declare the glory of God; the skies proclaim the work of His hands. Day after day they pour forth speech; night after night they display knowledge. There is no speech or language where their voice is not heard. Their voice goes out into all the earth, their words to the ends of the world." -- Psalm 19:1-4

WHY GO TO CHURCH?

If you're spiritually alive, you're going to love this! If you're spiritually dead, you won't want to read it. If you're spiritually curious, there is still hope!

A Church goer wrote a letter to the editor of a newspaper and complained that it made no sense to go to church every Sunday. "I've gone for 30 years now," he wrote, "and in that time I have heard something like 3,000 sermons. But for the life of me, I can't remember a single one of them. So, I think I'm wasting my time and the pastors are wasting theirs by giving sermons at all."

This started a real controversy in the "Letters to the Editor" column, much to the delight of the editor. It went on for weeks until someone wrote this clincher:

"I've been married for 30 years now. In that time my wife has cooked some 32,000 meals. But, for the life of me, I cannot recall the entire menu for a single one of those meals. But I do know this... They all nourished me and gave me the strength I needed to do my work.

If my wife had not given me these meals, I would be physically dead today. Likewise, if I had not gone to church for nourishment, I would be spiritually dead today!"

When you are DOWN to nothing, God is UP to something! Faith sees the invisible, believes the incredible and receives the impossible!

Thank God for your physical AND our spiritual nourishment! When Satan is knocking at your door, simply say, "Jesus, could you get that for me?"

THE FIVE FINGER PRAYER

Use Your Fingers when you Pray

1. Thumb (people who are close to you)
Your thumb is nearest to you. So begin your prayers by praying for those closest to you. They are the easiest to remember. To pray for our loved ones is, as C.S. Lewis once said, a "sweet duty".

2. Pointer (people who point the way)
The next finger is the pointing finger. Pray for those who teach, instruct and heal. This includes teachers, doctors, and ministers. They need support and wisdom in pointing others in the right direction. Keep them in your prayers.

3. Tall Finger (people in authority)

The next finger is the tallest finger. It reminds us of our leaders. Pray for the president, leaders in business and industry, and administrators. These people shape our nation and guide public opinion. They need God's guidance.

4. Ring Finger (people who are weak)

The fourth finger is our ring finger. Surprising to many is the fact that this is our weakest finger; as any piano teacher will testify. It should remind us to pray for those who are weak, in trouble or in pain. They need your prayers day and night. You cannot pray too much for them.

5. Little Finger (your own needs)

And lastly comes our little finger; the smallest finger of all. Which is where we should place ourselves in relation to God and others. As the Bible says, "the least shall be the greatest among you." Your pinky should remind you to pray for yourself.

By the time you have prayed for the other four groups, your own needs will be put into proper perspective and you will be able to pray for yourself more effectively.

Use your daily routine of life to reinforce your prayer life:
When you first wake up - Praise your Creator
When you shower or bathe - Ask for cleansing of your soul; confess, repent & receive forgiveness

When you eat - Give thanks not only for the food, but for your family, home, life, etc.
When you go to work or school - Pray for those with whom you come into contact

Where to Pray...

Jesus tells us where to pray in Matthew 6:6: "But

when you pray, go into your room, close the door and pray to your Father, who is unseen. Then your Father, who sees what is done in secret, will reward you."

How to Pray...

In Matthew 6:9-15 Jesus tells us how to pray when He gives us the pattern for prayer in what is now referred to as the Lord's prayer.

"This, then, is how you should pray:"

'Our Father in heaven, hallowed be your name, your kingdom come, your will be done on earth as it is in heaven. Give us today our daily bread. Forgive us our debts, as we also have forgiven our debtors. And lead us not into temptation, but deliver us from the evil one. 'For if you forgive men when they sin against you, your heavenly Father will also forgive you. But if you do not forgive men their sins, your Father will not forgive your sins."

ACHIEVING HAPPINESS WITH SELFISHNESS

There is this story of a man who had a dream one night. He dreamed that he died and found himself immediately in a large room. In the room there was a huge banquet table filled with all sorts of delicious foods. Around the table people were seated who were hungry but the chairs were five feet from the edge of the table and people apparently could not get out of the chairs and their arms were not long enough to reach the food. In the dream there was a single large spoon, five feet long. Everyone was fighting, quarrelling, and pushing each other, trying to grab hold of that spoon.

Finally in that awful scene, one strong bully got hold of the spoon. He reached out, picked up some food, and turned it to feed himself. Only to find out that the spoon was so long that as he held it out he could not touch his mouth.

The food fell off. Immediately someone else grabbed the spoon. Again, the person reached far enough to pick up the food, but could not feed himself. In the dream, the man was observing it all said to his guide, “this is hell-to have food and not be able to eat it”.

The guide replied, “Where do you think u are?

This is hell. But this is not our place. Come with me.”

And they went into another room. In this room things were the same as the previous room. People were not able to reach food coz of the same reasons. Yet they had a satisfied, pleasant look on their faces. Only then the visitors see the reason why. Exactly as before, there was only one spoon. It, too, had a handle five feet long. Yet no one was fighting for it. In fact, one man, who held the handle, reached out, picked up the food, and put it into the mouth of someone else, which ate it and was satisfied.

That person then took the spoon by the handle, reached for the food from the table, and put it back to the mouth of the man who had just given him something to eat. And the guide said, "This is heaven".

People who try to achieve happiness with selfishness end up it in a hell on earth. If u live by the laws of God and choose to look for people who have burdens, you might be able to help them. But if you look for our own happiness, ignoring the needs of those around u, u will lose out altogether.

There is this story of a man who had a dream one night. He dreamed that he died and found himself immediately in a large room. In the room there was a huge banquet table filled with all sorts of delicious foods. Around the table people were seated who were hungry but the chairs were five feet from the edge of the table and people apparently could not get out of the chairs and their arms were not long enough to reach the food. In the dream there was a single large spoon, five feet long. Everyone was fighting, quarrelling, and pushing each other, trying to grab hold of that spoon. Finally in that awful scene, one strong bully got hold of the spoon. He reached out, picked up some food, and turned it to feed himself. Only to find out that the spoon was so long that as he held it out he could not touch his mouth. The food fell off. Immediately someone else grabbed the spoon. Again, the person reached far enough to pick up the food, but could not feed himself. In the dream, the man was observing it all said to his guide, "this is hell-to have food and not be able to eat it".

The guide replied, "Where does u think u are? This is hell. But this is not our place. Come with me."

And they went into another room. In this room things were the same as the previous room. People were not able to reach food coz of the same reasons. Yet they had a satisfied, pleasant look on their faces. Only then the visitors see the reason why. Exactly as before, there was only one spoon. It, too, had a handle five feet long. Yet no one was fighting for it. In fact, one man, who held the handle, reached out, picked up the food, and put it into the mouth of someone else, which ate it and was satisfied. That person then took the spoon by the handle, reached for the food from the table, and put it back to the mouth of the man who had just given him something to eat. And the guide said, "This is heaven". People who try to achieve happiness with selfishness end up it in a hell on earth. If u live by the laws of God and choose to look for people who have burdens, you might be able to help them. But if you look for our own happiness, ignoring the needs of those around u, u will lose out altogether. There is this story of a man who had a dream one night. He dreamed that he died and found himself immediately in a large room. In the room there was a huge banquet table filled with all sorts of delicious foods. Around the table people were seated who were hungry but the chairs were five feet from the edge of the table and people apparently could not get out of the chairs and their arms were not long enough to reach the food. In the dream there was a single large spoon, five feet long. Everyone was fighting, quarrelling, and pushing each other, trying to grab hold of that spoon. Finally in that awful scene, one strong bully got hold of the spoon. He reached out, picked up some food, and turned it to feed himself. Only to find out that the spoon was so long that as he held it out he could not touch his mouth. The food fell off. Immediately someone else grabbed the spoon. Again, the person reached far enough to pick up the food, but could not feed himself. In the dream, the man was observing it all said to his guide, "this is hell-to have food and not be able to eat it". The guide replied, "Where do u think u are? This is hell. But this is not our place. Come with me." And they went into another room. In this room things were the same as the previous room. People were not able to reach food coz of the same reasons. Yet they had a satisfied, pleasant look on their faces.

Only then the visitors see the reason why. Exactly as before, there was only one spoon. It, too, had a handle five feet long. Yet no one was fighting for it. In fact, one man, who held the handle, reached out, picked up the food, and put it into the mouth of someone else, which ate it and was satisfied. That person then took the spoon by the handle, reached for the food from the table, and put it back to the mouth of the man who had just given him something to eat. And the guide said, "This is heaven". People who try to achieve happiness with selfishness end up it in a hell on earth. If u live by the laws of God and choose to look for people who have burdens, you might be able to help them. But if u look for our own happiness, ignoring the needs of those around u, u will lose out altogether.

NESTLE NOT WRESTLE

I watched Billy Graham being interviewed by Oprah Winfrey on television. Oprah told him that in her childhood home, she use to watch him preach on a little black and white TV while sitting on a linoleum floor.

She went on to the tell viewers that, in his lifetime, Billy has preached to twenty-million people around the world, not to mention the countless numbers who have heard him whenever his crusades are broadcast. When she asked if he got nervous before facing a crowd, Billy replied humbly, "No, I don't get nervous before crowds, but I did today before I was going to meet with you." Oprah's show is broadcast to twenty-million people every day. She is comfortable with famous stars and celebrities but seemed in awe of Dr. Billy Graham.

When the interview ended, she told the audience, "You don't often see this on my show, but we're going to pray." Then she asked Billy to close in prayer. The camera panned the studio audience as they bowed their heads and closed their eyes just like in one of his crusades.

Oprah sang the first line from the song that is his hallmark "Just as I am, without a plea," misreading the line and singing off-key, but her voice was full of emotion and almost cracked.

When Billy stood up after the show, instead of hugging her guest, Oprah's usual custom, she went over and just nestled against him. Billy wrapped his arm around her and pulled her under his shoulder. She stood in his fatherly embrace with a look of sheer contentment.

I once read the book "Nestle, Don't Wrestle" by Corrie Ten Boom. The power of nestling was evident on the TV screen that day. Billy Graham was not the least bit condemning, distant, or hesitant to embrace a public personality who may not fit the evangelistic mould. His grace and courage are sometimes stunning.

In an interview with Hugh Downs, on the 20/20 program, the subject turned to homosexuality. Hugh looked directly at Billy and said, "If you had a homosexual child, would you love him?" Billy didn't miss a beat. He replied with sincerity and gentleness, "Why, I would love that one even more." The title of Billy's autobiography, "Just as I Am," says it all. His life goes before him speaking as eloquently as that charming southern drawl for which he is known. If, when I am eighty years old, my autobiography were to be titled "Just As I Am," I wonder how I would live now? Do I have the courage to be me? I'll never be a Billy Graham, the elegant man who draws people to the Lord through a simple one-point message, but I hope to be a person who is real and compassionate and who might draw people to nestle within God's embrace. Do you make it a point to speak to a visitor or person who shows up alone at church, buy a hamburger for a homeless man, call your mother on Sunday afternoons, pick daisies with a little girl, or take a fatherless boy to a baseball game? Did anyone ever tell you how beautiful you look when you're looking for what's beautiful in someone else? Billy complimented Oprah when asked what he was most thankful for; he said, "Salvation given to us in Jesus Christ" then added, "and the way you have made people all over this country aware of the power of being grateful. "When asked his secret of love, being married fifty-four years to the same person, he said, "Ruth and I are happily incompatible. “How unexpected. We would all live more comfortably with everybody around us if we would find the strength in being grateful and happily incompatible. Let's take the things that set us apart, that make us different, that cause us to disagree, and make them an occasion to compliment each other and be thankful for each other. Let us be big enough to be smaller than our neighbour, spouse, friends, and strangers .Every day, may we "Nestle, not Wrestle!"

BLESSINGS FROM GIVING

Three young men were once given three kernels of corn apiece by a wise old sage, who admonished them to go out into the world, and use the corn to bring themselves good fortune. The first young man put his three kernels of corn into a bowl of hot broth and ate them. The second thought, I can do better than that, and he planted his three kernels of corn. Within a few months, he had three stalks of corn. He took the ears of corn from the stalks, boiled them, and had enough corn for three meals. The third man said to himself, I can do better than that! He also planted his three kernels of corn, but when his three stalks of corn produced, he stripped one of the stalks and replanted all of the seeds in it, gave the second stalk of corn to a sweet maiden, and ate the third. His one full stalk's worth of replanted corn kernels gave him 200 stalks of corn! And the kernels of these he continued to replant, setting aside only a bare minimum to eat. He eventually planted a hundred acres of corn. With his fortune, he not only won the hand of the sweet maiden but purchased the land owned by the sweet maiden's father. And he never hungered again. It is possible to give freely to GOD and become more wealthy, but those who are stingy will lose everything. The generous prosper and are satisfied; those who refresh others will themselves be refreshed. – Proverbs 11:24-25

CHRISTMAS BOOTS AND SHOES

Bobby was getting cold sitting out in his back yard in the snow. Bobby didn't wear boots; he didn't like them and anyway he didn't own any. The thin sneakers he wore had a few holes in them and they did a poor job of keeping out the cold.

Bobby had been in his backyard for about an hour already. And, try as he might, he could not come up with an idea for his mother's Christmas gift. He shook his head as he thought, "This is useless, even if I do come up with an idea, and I don't have any money to spend."Ever since his father had passed away three years ago, the family of five had struggled. It wasn't because his mother didn't care, or try, there just never seemed to be enough. She worked nights at the hospital, but the small wage that she was earning could only be stretched so far.

What the family lacked in money and material things, they more than made up for in love and family unity. Bobby had two older and one younger sister, who ran the household in their mother's absence. All three of his sisters had already made beautiful gifts for their mother.

Somehow it just wasn't fair. Here it was Christmas Eve already, and he had nothing.

Wiping a tear from his eye, Bobby kicked the snow and started to walk down to the street where the shops and stores were. It wasn't easy being six without a father, especially when he needed a man to talk to. Bobby walked from shop to shop, looking into each decorated window. Everything seemed so beautiful and so out of reach. It was starting to get dark and Bobby reluctantly turned to walk home when suddenly his eyes caught the glimmer of the setting sun's rays reflecting off of something along the curb. He reached down and discovered a shiny dime. Never before has anyone felt so wealthy as

Bobby felt at that moment. As he held his new found treasure, a warmth spread throughout his entire body and he walked into the first store he saw. His excitement quickly turned cold when salesperson after salesperson told him that he could not buy anything with only a dime.

He saw a flower shop and went inside to wait in line. When the shop owner asked if he could help him, Bobby presented the dime and asked if he could buy one flower for his mother's Christmas gift. The shop owner looked at Bobby and his ten cent offering. Then he put his hand on Bobby's shoulder and said to him, "You just wait here and I'll see what I can do for you."

As Bobby waited, he looked at the beautiful flowers and even though he was a boy, he could see why mothers and girls liked flowers.

The sound of the door closing as the last customer left jolted Bobby back to reality. All alone in the shop, Bobby began to feel alone and afraid.

Suddenly the shop owner came out and moved to the counter. There, before Bobby's eyes, lay twelve long stem, red roses, with leaves of green and tiny white flowers all tied together with a big silver bow. Bobby's heart sank as the owner picked them up and placed them gently into a long white box.

"That will be ten cents young man." the shop owner said reaching out his hand for the dime. Slowly, Bobby moved his hand to give the man his dime. Could this be true? No one else would give him a thing for his dime! Sensing the boy's reluctance, the shop owner added, "I just happened to have some roses on sale for ten cents a dozen. Would you like them? "This time Bobby did not hesitate, and when the man placed the long box into his hands, he knew it was true. Walking out the door that the owner was holding for Bobby, he heard the shop keeper say, "Merry Christmas, son." As he returned inside, the shop keepers' wife walked out. "Who were you talking to back there and where are the roses you were fixing?" Staring out the window, and blinking the tears from his own eyes, he replied, "A strange thing happened to me this morning. While I was setting up things to open the shop, I thought I heard a voice telling me to set aside a dozen of my best roses for a special gift. I wasn't sure at the time whether I had lost my mind or what, but I set them aside anyway. Then just a few minutes ago, a little boy came into the shop and wanted to buy a flower for his mother with one small dime. "When I looked at him, I saw myself, many years ago. I too, was a poor boy with nothing to buy my mother a Christmas gift. A bearded man, whom I never knew, stopped me on the street and told me that he wanted to give me ten dollars. "When I saw that little boy tonight, I knew who that voice was, and I put together a dozen of my very best roses." The shop owner and his wife hugged each other tightly, and as they stepped out into the bitter cold air, they somehow didn't feel cold at all.

A WHIP IN HIS HAND

Compassion is not having a bleeding heart full of sympathy for others -- compassion is such a depth of love that one is willing to do whatever it takes to bring awareness to a situation. Let me remind you of a situation that happened in Jesus' life. He took a whip and entered the great temple of Jerusalem. A whip in the hand of Jesus? Yes, Jesus can handle a whip, no problems; the whip cannot overpower him. He remains alert, his consciousness is such.

The great temple of Jerusalem had become a place of robbers. A subtle robbery was going on.

There were money changers inside the temple, and they were exploiting the whole country.

Jesus entered their temple alone and upturned their boards -- the boards of the money changers -- threw their money and created such turmoil that the moneychangers escaped outside the temple. They were many and Jesus was alone, but he was in such a fury, in such a fire! Now, how do we explain this? Jesus is the dove, a man of peace.

How could he take a whip in his hands? How could he be so angry, so enraged, that he upturned the boards of the moneychangers and threw the moneychangers out of the temple? And his energy must have been in a storm.

They could not face him. The priests and the business people and the moneychangers all escaped, shouting, "This man has gone mad!"

Jesus is absolutely innocent! He is not violent. He is not destructive. It is his compassion.

It is his love. The whip in his hands is the whip in the hands of love.

A PENNY

Several years ago, a friend of mine and her husband were invited to spend the weekend at the husband's employer's home. My friend, Arlene, was nervous about the weekend. The boss was very wealthy, with a fine home on the waterway, and cars costing more than her house. The first day and evening went well, and Arlene was delighted to have this rare glimpse into how the very wealthy live. The husband's employer was quite generous as a host, and took them to the finest restaurants. Arlene knew she would never have the opportunity to indulge in this kind of extravagance again, so was enjoying herself immensely. As the three of them were about to enter an exclusive restaurant that evening, the boss was walking slightly ahead of Arlene and her husband. He stopped suddenly, looking down on the pavement for a long, silent moment. Arlene wondered if she was supposed to pass him. There was nothing on the ground except a single darkened penny that someone had dropped, and a few cigarette butts. Still silent, the man reached down and picked up the penny.

He held it up and smiled, then put it in his pocket as if he had found a great treasure. How absurd! What need did this man have for a single penny? Why would he even take the time to stop and pick it up? Throughout dinner, the entire scene nagged at her. Finally, she could stand it no longer.

She causally mentioned that her daughter once had a coin collection, and asked if the penny he had found had been of some value. A smile crept across the man's face as he reached into his pocket for the penny and held it out for her to see. She had seen many pennies before!

What was the point of this?

"Look at it." He said. "Read what it says."

She read the words "United States of America."

"No, not that; read further."

"One cent?"

"No, keep reading."

"In God we Trust?"

"Yes! "And?"

"And if I trust in God, the name of God is holy, even on a coin. Whenever I find a coin I see that inscription. It is written on every single United States coin, but we never seem to notice it! God drops a message right in front of me telling me to trust Him? Who am I to pass it by? When I see a coin, I pray, I stop to see if my trust IS in God at that moment. I pick the coin up as a response to God; that I do trust in Him.

For a short time, at least, I cherish it as if it were gold. I think it is God's way of starting a conversation with me. Lucky for me, God is patient and pennies are plentiful!

When I was out shopping today, I found a penny on the sidewalk. I stopped and picked it up, and realized that I had been worrying and fretting in my mind about things I cannot change. I read the words, "In God We Trust," and had to laugh. Yes, God, I get the message.

It seems that I have been finding an inordinate number of pennies in the last few months, but then, pennies are plentiful!

And, God is patient...

Have a blessed day!!

The best mathematical equation I have ever seen:

1 cross + 3 nails -------- 4 given

A PRAYER OF A DYING CHILD

I woke up one morning and I was 17,
I knew the day had come
The day I prove to everyone how cool I was
The day I accepted death as my destiny

Little did I know I would regret that day
And my family who kept me alive for 17 years
Would be cursed by me for years of never ending pain

Without thinking I lit the cigarette
I knew it had to be done before the day was over
I coughed a little but I was fine
Now as I lay in bed coughing and choking
My family is beside me

My parents and my sister

I whisper in my sister's ear
"Please don't do what I did"
She just nodded her head in silence

Now as my angel holds me in his arms
I know it's time for me to go
I close my eyes and kiss him one last time
It's funny how we resent those who try to help us when we're alive
And how we beg them to save us when we're about to die
All this because of one silly cigarette
All this because someone was dumb enough to say that Smoking is cool

FORGIVE ME WHEN I WHINE

Today, upon a bus,
I saw a girl with golden hair.
I envied her, she seemed so gay,
And I wished I was as fair.
When suddenly she rose to leave,
I saw her hobble down the aisle.
She had one leg and used a crutch.
But as she passed, she gave a smile.

Oh, God, forgive me when I whine.
I have 2 legs, the world is mine.

I stopped to buy some candy.
The lad who sold it had such charm.
I talked with him, he seemed so glad.
If I were late, it'd do no harm.

And as I left, he said to me,
"I thank you, you've been so kind.
It's nice to talk with folks like you.
You see," he said, "I'm blind."

Oh, God, forgive me when I whine.

I have 2 eyes, the world is mine.
Later while walking down the street,
I saw a child with eyes of blue.
He stood and watched the others play.
He seemed not to know what to do.

I stopped a moment and then I said,
"Why don't you join the others dear?"
He looked ahead without a word.
And then I knew he couldn't hear.

Oh, God, forgive me when I whine.
I have 2 ears, the world is mine.
With feet to take me where I'd go.

With eyes to see the sunset's glow.
With ears to hear what I'd know.
Oh, God, forgive me when I whine
I've been blessed indeed, the world is mine.

A MIRACLE

Like any good mother, when Karen found out that another baby was on the way, she did what she could to help her 3-year-old son, Michael, prepare for a new sibling. They found out that the new baby was going to be a girl, and day after day, night after night, Michael sang to his sister in Mommy's tummy. The pregnancy progressed normally for Karen, an active member of the Panther Creek United Methodist Church in Morristown, Tennessee. Then the labor pains came.

Every five minutes ... every minute. But complications arose during delivery. Hours of labour. Would a C-section be required? Finally, Michael's little sister was born. But she was in serious condition. With sirens howling in the night, the ambulance rushed the infant to the neonatal intensive care unit at St. Mary's Hospital, Knoxville,

Tennessee. The days inched by. The little girl became worse. The pediatric specialist told the parents to prepared for the worst. Karen and her husband contacted a local cemetery about a burial plot. They originally fixed up a special room in their home for the new baby - now they planned a funeral. Michael kept begging his parents to let him see his sister, "I want to sing to her," he said. Week two in intensive care. It looked as if a funeral would come before the week was over. Michael kept nagging about singing to his sister, but kids are not allowed in Intensive Care. Karen made up her mind. She decided to take Michael whether they like it or not. If he didn't see his sister now, he may never see her alive. She dressed him in an oversized scrub suit and marched him into ICU. He looked like a walking laundry basket, but the head nurse recognized him as a child and bellowed, "Get that kid out of here now! No children are allowed. The mother in Karen rose up strong, and the usually mild-mannered lady glared steel-eyed into the head nurse's face, her lips a firm line. "He is not leaving until he sings to his sister!" Karen towed Michael to his sister's bedside. He gazed at the tiny infant losing the battle to live. And he began to sing. In the pure hearted voice of a 3-year-old, Michael sang: "You are my sunshine, my only sunshine, you make me happy when skies are gray --- " Instantly the baby girl responded. The pulse rate became calm and steady. "Keep on singing, Michael." "You never know, dear, how much I love you, Please don't take my sunshine away---" Her strained breathing became smoother. "Keep on singing, Michael." "The other night, dear, as I lay sleeping, I dreamed I held you in my arms..." Michael's little sister relaxed as healing rest seemed to sweep over her.

"Keep on singing, Michael." Tears conquered the face of the bossy head nurse. "You are my sunshine, my only sunshine. Please don't, take my sunshine away."The next day--the very next day--the little girl was well enough to go home! Woman's Day magazine called it "The Miracle of a Brother's Song." The medical staff just called it a miracle. Karen called it a miracle of God's love.

E-BOOKS BY AUTHOR

- How to Get Motivated
- How to Plan For A New Career
- How to Develop Unstoppable Confidence
- Successful Interviews: Making The Most Of The Interview
- The Interview Guide: A Job Interview Is No Different Than Finding The Right Partner
- The Structure and Application of Cognitive Behavioural Therapy

- How to Think Critically
- Mentoring As A Workforce Development Strategy
- The Counselling Process In Six Stages: A Basic Guide For Psychologists Counsellors and Psychotherapists
- Linking Emotional Intelligence To Effective Leadership
- Stress Management
- A Critique Of Executive Coaching Through The Psychodynamic Window
- Otto Kernberg's Theory of

Personality: Pathological Narcissism and Borderline Personality Disorders

- Personality Development and Confidence Building
- The Psychology of the Courtroom
- How To Improve Your Communication Skills
- How Employment Assessment Centres Work
- Effective Presentations Skills
- Linking Emotional Intelligence To Effective Leadership

- Stress Management Leading Career Development and Employability
- The History of Psychological Testing
- How To Have A Bad Interview
- Have You Ever Thought of Becoming A Life Coach
- Successful Interviews
- The 360 Degree Feedback System Is By Far The Best Performance Assessment Tool By Far.

www.ingramcontent.com/pod-product-compliance
Ingram Content Group UK Ltd.
Pitfield, Milton Keynes, MK11 3LW, UK
UKHW020417250726
13967UKWH00007B/2689

9 781943 274512